# DAILY GRATITUDE

## *Reflections*

### VOLUME 2

## 365 Guides to Great-Full Living

# DEBORAH PERDUE

Published by
Applegate Valley Publishing
Grants Pass, Oregon
www.graceofgratitude.com

ISBN: 978-1-7370685-3-2

Design by Deborah Perdue of Illumination Graphics
www.illuminationgraphics.com

Photography courtesy of Deborah Perdue,
depositphotos.com, pixabay.com, unsplash.com
and shutterstock.com

# DEDICATION

*To all of the spiritual lightworkers*

*who assist in bringing more peace, joy and love*

*into the world.*

*And to all who are striving to awaken and help too.*

*Thank you!*

## Other Books by This Author

All of Deborah Perdue's books are available directly at the
author's website, GraceOfGratitude.com
or on Amazon.com

# A Thank You Gift Just for You

As a thank you, I am offering all of my readers a free gift.

I send out Daily Gratitude Reflections five days a week.
In them, I share some favorite inspirational quotes. Additionally,
I share uplifting and personal reflections for each day.

Below are some of the testimonials I have received. I believe these
Daily Gratitudes will prove to be an encouragement and blessing
to you as well.

*"The Daily Gratitude Reflections emails are a constant,
consistent reminder of how good life really is,
and I look forward to them greatly."*
J. Taylor

*"I look forward to reading your Daily inspirations every day and
appreciate the time you take to write and share them."*
K. Ray

*"Keep the vibrations of love flowing! The Daily Gratitude
Reflections are deep and wondrous, and touch my heart.*
P. Singh

You may email me at info@GraceOfGratitude.com to start
receiving Daily Gratitudes free to your inbox. There is no
obligation and you may unsubscribe at any time.

# Introduction

You are invited to use these Daily Gratitude Reflections on a daily basis. Start any time of the year, or right on New Year's Day. Or you can just pick a passage randomly, then watch how the Universe surprises you with the perfect one!

Gratitude is a huge passion for me, is an integral part of my life, and has grown since I first started consciously practicing being grateful in the early 2000s. It has exponentially improved my own life. I went from being a complainer and enjoying regular pity-parties for no reason, really, to realizing how nonproductive that was. Why not look at what is right, what is going well, rather than focusing on problems?! This was a revelation for me.

In the future, I intend to write a book called "Gratitude Beyond Reason" about practicing Radical Gratitude, because as my gratitude practice expands, it has become apparent to me that even in the toughest times of our lives, something to be thankful for can almost always be found. In my own life, for instance, I have seen that be true, when a wildfire was so close to our house we had to evacuate, and we ended up becoming "best friends" with a couple who took us in. There were other gratitude aha's too from the fire so near to us. And during the 2020 COVID times, which have been stressful and such a monumental change in our lives, I became familiar enough with Zoom technology to offer spiritual classes. Now I facilitate book study classes online, and have people from all over the United States attend. This would not have happened in "normal times."

Sometimes it feels like I am too repetitive, yet there are some important tenets in which I believe, and they do keep showing up in my gratitude reflections! My spiritual path, with all its twists and turns, brought me to discover the Centers for Spiritual Living in 1998, and since then, I deepen my faith every year. I firmly believe God is everywhere (as I was actually taught as a young girl with a Catholic upbringing). However, God is not a he or she, but omniscient. Each of us – all flora, all creatures, and every bit of nature and the stars beyond – are all part of this Presence. And God IS synonymous with love. With our free choice, we can create a heavenly life or a hellish existence. I choose love and peace and joy and harmony and beauty, and all the good stuff. So please forgive me for this repetition.

One of the people I most admire, Helen Keller, managed to find gratitude constantly, and chronicled it for us, despite her physical afflictions that would be too much for most people to handle. Viktor Frankl is another person I so admire, who survived the Holocaust, and consciously kept his spirits up, and wrote his monumental book *Man's Search for Meaning*. The Dalai Lama, although exiled from his beloved country Tibet, forgave the Chinese leaders who pushed him out, and lives in peace and love, despite what he has gone through and is now a venerated, positive, ever-so-joyful spiritual world leader. I strive to be a person like them! I strive to be forever optimistic, and to find the pearls of good even in bad times.

It has been seven years or more since I started writing Daily Gratitude Reflections to my email subscribers. The Reflections in this book are the cream of the crop from the last three years. Please enjoy them . . .

*Deborah Perdue*

## – DAY 1 –

*"The universe buries strange jewels deep within us all, and then stands back to see if we can find them."*
Elizabeth Gilbert

As I soul-search and keep evolving, I discover and excavate more and
more precious jewels within me.
Who I was in my twenties is not a reflection of who I am now.
I have become more extroverted, though I am still an introvert.
I keep finding facets of creativity to bring forth.
My ability to love has grown exponentially.
I am still a diamond in the rough but life is polishing me.
And yes, I am grateful.

## – DAY 2 –

*"With the opening of the New Year, all the closed portals of limitations will be thrown open, and I shall move through them to vaster fields, where my worthwhile dreams of life will be fulfilled."*
Paramahansa Yogananda

I throw my own arms open to let the vaster fields of my dreams
come into my life.
How amazing it is to always have more to wish for, more to accomplish,
more to manifest.
Life is not static, and it is a great gift that it's ever-changing and fluid.

I am incredibly grateful for all of this and so much more.

Thank you, Infinite Universe.

## – DAY 3 –

*"Soft, fluid and ever changing, a jellyfish surrenders to the ocean's drifts and currents . . . by letting go, it gets to where it needs to go. We can learn a lesson from the jellyfish: Soften, let go, be patient and you will get where you need to go. Surrender is powerful."*
Emily Silva

I embrace surrender and letting go even though that goes against the tenaciousness in me. I soften my assured stance and trust that Spirit leads me. I need not fight against any currents. I am right where I need to be in every moment.

I am grateful for this wisdom. I am grateful for letting God and letting go.

## – DAY 4 –

*"You are loved just for being who you are, just for existing. You don't have to do anything to earn it. Your shortcomings, your lack of self-esteem, physical perfection, or social and economic success – none of that matters. No one can take this love away from you, and it will always be here."*
Ram Dass

Oh, to remember this every second of my life!
I am eternally grateful for every minute that I DO know and realize the truth of the inherent love that is the truth of life, of me,
of every single bit of life.
Let me love without measure.
And let me love myself as much as those I adore.
Let me love, love and then love some more.
Thank you.

## – DAY 5 –

*"People deal too much with the negative, with what is wrong. Why not try and see positive things, to just touch those things and make them bloom?"*
Thich Nhat Hanh

I am resolute in my devotion to the beauty, the compassion, the harmony of life. I envision deep peace, and pivot away from any lack.

Doing so, I nurture the blooming that opens my heart and soul, rather than what mutes my zest.

LIFE IS TRULY SO BREATHTAKINGLY BEAUTIFUL
and I am grateful beyond reason for that.

## – DAY 6 –

*"Back of our smallest act is the strength of the Universe.*
*Behind all our thoughts is the Infinite Thinker.*
*Diffused through every human activity is the Divine Presence."*
Ernest Holmes

Wow! I sometimes find this hard to believe, going into doubt or fear, however, I shore up my faith and trust in this knowing.

I tap into the Divine strength and guidance every single day, religiously.

I ward off thoughts of how this couldn't be possible
looking at the state of the world and some people's actions,
yet I know without an iota of doubt that Oneness is the truth of life
and in that Oneness, we can know it all and I am deeply thankful.

You know how sometimes things go wrong, and then we are very disappointed and dismayed?

When things happen where I am let down, I can feel hopeless, as if there is a big blockade in front of me.

What I am grateful for is how when roadblocks happen in my life, (after I go through the process of disappointment and grief), then like a phoenix, I DO rise from the ashes, filled with new energy and enthusiasm and motivation to try, try again!

I am thankful for my stick-to-it-ness!

## – DAY 8 –

Sometimes I feel like a broken record, repeating grateful, positive ideas and messages over and over and over.

Yet, as a society don't we bang the drum time and time again on what is wrong, what is not working?

I'm speaking of a prevailing, ongoing commentary of lack, scarcity, disease, nature catastrophes, war, domination – all with the predominating feeling of FEAR.

So consider my messages a healing balm.
I proudly and firmly bang my dream for love, peace, harmony, plenty, well-being, joy and all-good.
It is a steady, insistent beat, and I do not apologize. Forever thankful.

## – DAY 9 –

*"Do not be dismayed by the darkness of the world. All things break. And all things can be mended. Not with time, as they say, but with intention. So go. Love intentionally, extravagantly, unconditionally. The broken world waits in darkness for the light that is you."*
L.R. Knost

I find great solace in the quote above as so much appears to be not right on Earth. And with all my heart, I wish to shine my loving light on all I encounter. I am thankful to stand for peace and to walk the talk too.

Darkness can always be dissipated completely with light. Sow love instead of hate. Have compassion for even those who seem to be snuffing out the light. I am grateful for every bright-light wayshowers on this planet, myself included.

## – DAY 10 –

*"The intuitive mind is a sacred gift and the rational mind is a faithful servant. We have created a society that honors the servant and has forgotten the gift."*
Albert Einstein

I sometimes am guilty of forgetting the sacred gift of intuition.
And yet I know my intuition serves me in benevolent ways, when I trust it.
It is all-knowing and omniscient.
When we are intuitive, we are tapping into the Divine mind.
It takes listening and paying attention, not letting it be drowned out by facts and rationalizations.
Intuition is quiet, and I find that the logical, rational mind can shout at me.
Thank you, Great Spirit, for the plethora of gifts you bestow upon all of us and let us use them for all good.

## – DAY 11 –

*"I urge you all, fervently I urge you, to state unto the universe, unto the multiverse: I AM, I AM, I AM! I am life. I am God. I AM. As you state the knowingness within your breast, you raise your frequency. The vibration of I AM will begin to pulsate within you."*
St. Germain

I AM
love, peace, joy
compassion, serenity, light, harmony
balance, abundance, wholeness, well-being.
All that God is, I AM.

And how grateful I am!

## – DAY 12 –

*"Love is the sandpaper that takes away the harshness of intelligence."*
Paramahansa Yogananda

I am grateful to be filled with love, to come from the heart as much as I can, to love the world – all creatures great and small, all of nature, and all people whether they are dimly lit or brightly illuminated.

Love is the sandpaper that smooths out the rough spots of hurt and hatred that I may hold within me.

So thankful to listen to my heart rather than my logical mind, and let myself be open and warm-hearted.

Love lights up my life!

# – DAY 13 –

*"If you keep holding on to something after it's time to let go,*
*you'll end up with emotional rope burns."*
Linda Salazar

How grateful I am to have learned to release and forgive people and
events that bother me,
rather than clinging to my resentment or upset.

I am thankful to enjoy an unhampered clear mind and heart
without this type of emotional baggage weighing me down.

# – DAY 14 –

*"The soul wants to grow."*
Deborah Perdue

Although I much prefer routine and the same ol' same ol', I know my soul
is always seeking to expand my consciousness and it will have its way,
sometimes as I attempt to cling fiercely to what has been before.

And yet, I am a mind explorer, a soul adventurer, a spiritual spelunker, and
I watch as new experiences are conjured up
to help me be a deeper, wiser version of myself.

Deeply grateful for spiritual evolution, which actually brings me closer
to the true me.

## – DAY 15 –

Grace flows in and grace flows out . . .

I am supremely grateful for those times I know and feel that I am graced
and blessed.

Today happens to be a day where everything is flowing so sweetly;
where I feel absolute joy simply gazing at the lovely sky and trees nearby;
where I feel that gracious peace permeating my heart and soul.

Thank you, God–Goddess–All-That-Is
for life itself.

## – DAY 16 –

I am thankful when I realize that I am in control of myself
and not much else.

Knowing this, I can relax and allow and surrender
to things and people that go a way that might not be my preference.

And how I appreciate knowing that I can choose differently
if I don't like what is going on within me –
and for the realization that my higher self is ultimately in charge of me,
and choices made from ego can take a backseat to Spirit,
as I grow in wisdom.

In gratitude for beneficial choices!

## – DAY 17 –

*"We do not heal the past by dwelling there; we heal the past by living fully in the present."*
Marianne Williamson

It is almost trite to talk about living in the moment.
Yet, therein truly lies a wellspring of joy, peace, wisdom and an expansive sense of well-being.

I am certainly not immune to rehashing what has transpired!
And I jump into the future rather too easily as well.
But within the gift of the present lies perfection.

Every moment we are okay. Every moment lets us know that, if we relax rambling thoughts and pause to feel it. I am thankful for the infinity of every now moment!

## – DAY 18 –

I am grateful for light sparkling through the clouds,
even in the darkness of winter.
The beauty of this time of year may not be as profusely showy, like spring,
it is more subtle, yet it beckons to me.

I am grateful for more naps and rest during this time of year
as I honor the silence, the stillness, the hibernation of animals and flora,
and allow my self downtime.

How grand and glorious are vast skies!

How grand and glorious are all the gifts I am given continually.

Completely thankful.

*"Our deepest fear is not that we are inadequate. Our deepest fear
is that we are powerful beyond measure.
It is our light, not our darkness that most frightens us."*
Marianne Williamson

Some of my life I didn't feel powerful, instead I felt powerless and
dependent upon outside forces.
Later I shrank from my own power, and was timid and played small.
Today I am grateful to own and feel the power of my being!
There is nothing I can't accomplish with determination, creativity
and courage.
I know I am powerful beyond measure, with the help of my Higher Power,
and I am so thankful this is so.

**– DAY 20 –**

I believe in, and feel a connection to the other side – to life beyond
this world, through the thin veil
that we sometimes don't know how to penetrate.
I am grateful to lift the veil and feel the presence of my angels
and devoted guides on the other side, who are without a doubt,
my cheerleaders and Divine assistants.

And I've learned to ask for assistance, which the angels gladly give.

I take time each morning to listen and I receive messages.
They are always working on my behalf, for my highest good.
And I am deeply grateful for this celestial connection!

## – DAY 21 –

*"If your compassion does not include yourself, it is incomplete."*
Jack Kornfield

It is so much easier to love others than to truly love myself.
I am so grateful when I am able to hold myself in the highest regard; love myself immeasurably; forgive myself as readily as I forgive others.

Watching myself growing in self-love as the years go by, I am thankful.

And I am grateful for every time I catch myself in negative self-talk so I can transform those words into appreciation instead.

Just like everyone, I am a work in progress, and I celebrate my kindness toward myself, and all other sentient beings.

## – DAY 22 –

*"The mind becomes a friend to the one who has control over it and an enemy to the one who is controlled by it."*
Edward Viljoen

So very grateful for learning how to have more control over my thoughts, which can run amuck, and are certainly not always peaceful or kind.
How fabulous to have a spiritual path that shows me how to override automatic negativity, to be still and know.

I am thankful for the time I gift myself each morning in meditation and contemplation – what an invaluable gift is stillness.

I celebrate peace and calm and my deliberate pivoting toward gratitude and positivity.

## – DAY 23 –

So thankful for the happy home where I abide . . .
with forests and rivers and clear blue skies surrounding us,
with cherished pets that delight me in their company every single day . . .
our happy home is the retreat I come home to whenever I am away.

And more than that, I abide in my own happy home,
the one that is within me, the place that always offers comfort
and quiet solace as I commune with the Oneness that is deep within me
and all around me.

Home is where the heart is
and I am deeply grateful.

## – DAY 24 –

It is said, and I believe, that when one door closes, another opens.

How thankful I am that I am willing to enter new territory
even when I've never ventured there before.

I am supremely grateful for the courage, inner strength
and resilience I possess.

It bides me well when the old and familiar is over,
and it's time to move on.
I can accept it and feel trust that I am supported, guided
and always taken care of.

That which I am seeking is also seeking me and we find each other!

*"I commit to being a channel of God's love.
I am here to radiate peace, well-being and calm.
No matter what I face, I see through the surface conditions
to the great reality of love."*
Rev. Dr. Michael Gott

Without a doubt, I know I am love, I am loved, I am loving.
How great it is to feel this, to embody this, to be this now.
I am grateful beyond measure to realize that love conquers all, including
its arch enemy fear.
Love flows through me, to me, and from me.
How thankful am I.

## – DAY 26 –

*"Illumination comes from within and reflects outward.
Sleep offers the time to recharge your inner light.
Offer gratitude and fall asleep knowing that this light is always glowing
as you recharge your sparkle."*
Emily Silva

How grateful I am to let gratitude wash over me, even as I slumber.

I start my day with feeling grateful and fall asleep
counting my many blessings.

I am glad to glow with gratitude, and shine my love and light
everywhere I go.

## – DAY 27 –

*"Feelings come and go like clouds in a windy sky.*
*Conscious breathing is my anchor."*
Thich Nhat Hanh

Again and again, I watch my feelings grab me,
and if they are not particularly positive, I can feel stuck in them.

How grateful am I to witness them, breathe into the present moment,
and watch them float by, intermittent and illusive.

I am eternally thankful for my spiritual practices,
which really can be as simple as breathing mindfully.

## – DAY 28 –

*"The heart of most spiritual practice is simply this – remember.*
*Remember who you are."*
Wayne Mueller

I am grateful for all the times I remember!
Sometimes losing perspective with day-to-day drama and upset,
but oftentimes, more and more, remembering that we are way more
than our bodies, so much more than what defines our lives on Earth.
I remember that my spirit is light and free.
I remember that love is the most important power in the universe!
I remember that I am love, and I express love in all I do
and in my relationships.

I remember often, and I am deeply thankful.

*"I find ecstasy in living – the mere sense of living is joy enough."*
Emily Dickinson

I constantly savor the exquisite beauty of my surroundings
and adore my family, furry friends, and all of the precious souls I know.

Being thankful is such a habit that I honestly don't take anything for
granted about this beautiful life.

There is darkness but I know the light always shines and blinds the dark.
A gazillion stars twinkle at night and that is a joy to behold too.
I am grateful for my ecstatic viewpoint, knowing all that I have and all that
I am is nothing short of magnificent.

## – DAY 30 –

*"Unconditional love really exists in all of us. It is part of our deep inner
being. It's love for no reason, love without an object.
It's just sitting in love, a love that incorporates the chair and the room and
permeates everything around. The thinking mind is extinguished in love."*
Ram Dass

May our hearts be filled with the love that extends to everything alive,
and that is everything!

May our hearts burst open with unconditional love
for ourselves, for each other and for the world.

I am very thankful for all the love in my life,
and especially, for the love I share.

## – DAY 31 –

*"Mistakes are about getting the blessing in the lesson
and the lesson is the blessing."*
Michael B. Beckwith

I am sincerely grateful for every mistake, for every misstep, for every
seeming wrong choice I have made in my entire life.
All steps, even backward steps, have helped me become the strong, light-
filled human being that I am.
And although wrong turns have been made, and sometimes I wish I could
have realized the way forward more quickly, I know that my life is filled with
blessings and I got here exactly because of every single choice I made.

I can truthfully state that I love myself, one of the greatest blessings.

## – DAY 32 –

*"In deep gratitude, I allow all the power of the whole Universe
to express as me!"*
Rev. Michelle Ingalls

I stand strong in power and strength of mind, body and heart.

I know that the Universe supports me in absolutely
everything I do, so I've got the power!

And I use this power for good.

Deeply thankful.

*"The more clearly we can focus our attention on the wonders and realities of the universe about us, the less taste we shall have for destruction."*
Rachel Carson

I am incredibly thankful for my understanding of the grandeur and splendor of the utter magic of the universe.

Not a day goes by that I lose the gratitude in my heart for life itself. And so, accordingly, I do my best not to cause physical or mental harm to anything. And I firmly believe that if we all truly understood how inter-connected we all are, peace would prevail. I pray to live in peace, shining it outward, and to witness world peace in my lifetime.

## – DAY 34 –

Thank you, Spirit, for my growing,
ever-evolving consciousness so that I am able to grasp more
of what is important in life, and let go of what is not.

I am grateful to realize that everything I experience comes from
how I perceive it, and I can always change my mind!

How powerful we truly are
when we let go of feeling like a victim
and let our true essence shine.

## – DAY 35 –

*"Sometimes grief and sadness drain our energy, leaving us with nothing to invest in the present moment.
But we can be kind even when we are tremendously sad."*
Edward Viljoen

Tragedies can, and usually do, bring out the very best in humankind. We rise to the occasion when disaster strikes, whether it is to our immediate friends or family or to those we don't even know.

I am grateful for the "kind" in humankind.

I am grateful for my own kind, giving heart
and I pray we all grow kinder in every single circumstance, not just moments of devastating loss.

## – DAY 36 –

Dear Soul,

Thank you. You stretch me to keep growing and knowing, and you offer me refuge and wisdom in this beautiful life.

I am grateful for the Divinity within me that is my soul essence,
past doubt and fear, past comparison,
past my ego worries and concerns.

I truly know on deep levels that I am healthy, wealthy, happy and free!
I am free in the Spirit and here to serve and love.

In total gratitude . . .
Deborah

*"The pain of life is pure salt; no more, no less. The amount of pain in life
remains the same, exactly the same. But the amount of bitterness we taste
depends on the container we put the pain in. So when you are in pain,
the only thing you can do is to enlarge your sense of things . . .
Stop being a glass. Become a lake."*
Mark Nepo

I am deeply thankful for the ability I have honed to open my heart, despite
grief or anger or abrasion. As I let pain in, I find it diffuses . . . if I try to
keep it out, my heart feels more like a dam, a barrier, about to break.
I am grateful to let myself be a lake, letting tears fall, facing all of the
enormity of life's disappointments and knowing the lake joins oceans, and
on and on, to infinity.

– DAY 38 –

*"I am perfect."*
Wilma Christian

This affirming statement was a wise elder's last words! Wow. How
inspiring that she believed this with all her heart on her deathbed.
One couldn't ask for more.

The truth is that even though we are flawed; even though we make mistakes;
even though we have ridden a bumpy and precarious road in life, because
we are One with All-That-Is, we are perfect – exactly as we are.
I am thankful to know that every life event has molded me into who I am,
and that I am truly perfect too.
Growing into this realization is a lifelong process. I am glad for all the time
I am given to know this more deeply.

*"May we each discover our own form of spiritual electricity –
and light up our world."*
Eileen Rivers

I am thankful for the passion I feel! I feel it for art, I feel it for writing and
reading. I feel it in the love I have for so many in my life.
I feel it for nature in all its forms.
I feel it in my work life (and I am so grateful to love what I do).
I have utmost passion for sharing gratitude with others, in every way I can.
I feel that passion when I teach and facilitate spiritual gatherings.
All of this causes sparks and sparkles within me . . .
causing metaphysical electricity
that I gladly share to join in lighting up our world.

# – DAY 40 –

*"That night, I knew that the infinite inside my physical body is just a
continuation of the infinite all around me.
I am part of the infinite, and so is every object I perceive."*
Don Miguel Ruiz

It is proven scientifically that each of us has stardust within our cells!
To me, this underscores the fact that we are all connected with everything
and everyone.
How grand, how amazing that everything is encompassed
in an infinite web of connectivity.

When I feel this deeply, I feel so much comfort and love and Oneness
that I lay every silly worry and fear aside. I am thankful for the love of the
universe, expanding and creating endlessly.

## – DAY 41 –

*"You have to find what sparks a light in you so that you in your own way can illuminate the world."*
Oprah Winfrey

Today, I celebrate light!
Light that illuminates and warms like a balmy summer day;
light that sparkles in the beautiful reflections found in water,
and in the night sky; light that shines from within us outward.

Let me be a bright light shining away darkness
in my own heart, and in the hearts of all I come in contact with.

I am so grateful for all the light shining in this universe within all realms
of existence.

## – DAY 42 –

I am thankful to be imperfectly perfect, or perfectly imperfect.
I love myself just the way I am, and just the way I am not.

Acceptance is key to self-love.
I am grateful to let go of blame or shame if I don't act in a way
that I would want to act,
or make a dreaded mistake. Oh dear!

I accept and cherish myself as I would a friend.

And self-love enables me to love others exponentially.

*"I've learned that I still have a lot to learn."*
Maya Angelou

How I appreciate every single year of my growing up to get to where I am today. And I am still growing up!
It takes a wise person to realize that she doesn't know as much as she thought she did. It's like learning a computer – for a while, I thought I was a big shot at it, and then realized how much more I could know and I got humble. Or when I was a teen and young adult, I had a know-it-all attitude and then as the school of life taught me, I was actually more ignorant than I realized. I am grateful to know I still have a lot to learn.
And I am grateful to life for offering an infinity of knowledge to dive into.

## – DAY 44 –

*"Today I look for the good and live in gratitude,*
*inviting abundance into every area of my life."*
Rev. Jane Beach

There is a powerful saying by Emma Curtis Hopkins,
**"PRAISE THE GOOD."**

Today I let myself see only the good in every situation and circumstance.

There are precious jewels to be found in all of life.

In gratitude, I open my heart to feel and accept the abundance of life in all its glory. I praise the good, and more good comes to me.

*"Ultimately, we have just one moral duty: to reclaim large areas of peace in ourselves, more and more peace, and to reflect it toward others. And the more peace there is in us, the more peace there will also be in our troubled world."*
Etty Hillesum

I bask in peace. Peace in my heart, peace in my soul, peace in my own inner sanctum. I welcome peace, I reclaim peace when I lose it, I emanate peace more and more.

It is a lifelong yearning of mine to see peace on this planet and I help it along by nurturing my own.
How grateful I am for inner peace, and love and compassion.

– DAY 46 –

*"I think 99 times and find nothing. I stop thinking, swim in silence, and the truth comes to me."*
Albert Einstein

Even a genius like Einstein realizes that thinking and overthinking can be counterproductive! As someone with dogged persistence, I know that I can chew on a thought like a dog bone, getting absolutely nowhere.

To let go; to be in the sacred silence, to meditate, to dream and ask for an answer yields rich results.

I am so thankful to realize that the left brain logical mind sometimes is in overdrive – and that to surrender and let go and trust instead is healing balm.

## – DAY 47 –

*"As coal under great pressure turns into a diamond,*
*our spirit under great pressure has the chance to turn into the jewel that it*
*is. This has always been known."*
Mark Nepo

Let me open to the chance to become more of the jewel that I truly am
every day, ever-increasingly.
Let me love, let me love exponentially.
Let me give, let me give in expansive, generous ways.
Let me be grateful for everything and everyone in my life.
There are infinite reasons to be grateful.
Let me see them all!
Thank you.

## – DAY 48 –

Today I shine God's love and light from my heart to the world!

And I am so thankful for the healing power of love.
I know that the love of God is omnipotent and when I open my heart,
I embody that powerful love which casts everything in the light of wonder
and beauty.

I am grateful for love of all kinds –
for self-love, which is the bridge to love others;
and for the love I share with family, and with friends;
for the love I have in my heart for all people, all animals, all of nature,
everything!

As I open my heart more and more, love rules my life.

## – DAY 49 –

*"Help me to be less fearful of the measure of time, and more fully alive in the time that simply is. Help me to live time, not just to simply use it; to breathe it in, and return it in acts of love and presence."*
Avis Crowe

I am so thankful when I slip into the present moment, letting go of what is to come and what has been.
That present moment is always perfect.
All is well.

I am grateful to breathe in the now, and to breathe out love and peace and harmony and deep faith, for others to share with me.

## – DAY 50 –

I stand strong on my mountaintop of peace, joy, love, light and positivity with its bedrock of faith, trust and serenity.

I am very grateful to hold my arms and heart open wide to receive all the blessings of the universe, as I circulate blessings, giving from my heart and soul.

The strength and power that my consciousness contains bides me well in outer world turmoil.

I invite you to stand strong with me!

## – DAY 51 –

I so appreciate flowing days where all is right in my world,
and living is easy.

I celebrate today, which is like that!
It feels like there is a gentle breeze of grace and ease blowing.

I am grateful for a peace-filled mind and heart, which nurtures
comfort and harmony.

And when things are out of sorts, I am grateful to know
that this too shall pass.

All is truly well.

## – DAY 52 –

*"Life is as fleeting as a rainbow, a flash of lightning, a star at dawn.*
*Knowing this, how can you quarrel?"*
Jack Kornfield

When someone passes that I know, especially when unexpected, it is SO
shocking. One day I talk to them or visit with them, and then suddenly,
they are gone.
Every time this happens, I realize how fleeting our time here truly is.
Death, like life, is imminent and we can't fight it.
What we can do is live life to the fullest,
making sure each item on our bucket list is checked off,
living life with gusto and zeal and appreciation.
My gratitude practice helps me stay in joy and peace and enthusiasm.
Life is good, and I'm grateful, every single day, to live it!

*"Every curve of the road is guiding you. Every tree knows your footfall.*
*Every bit of sky is whispering clues to you.*
*A Mysterious, Brilliant Love is drawing you forward, rooting for you,*
*investing in you, chanting for your fruition."*
Tama Kieves

How grand it is to feel assured that we are always being guided, supported
and connected with the Universe/The Great Creator/Our Higher Power.
I feel this deeply in meditation.
I observe that every circumstance in my life is leading me on to more
wisdom, more knowledge, more love.
God whispers in the stillness, and I am so thankful to listen.

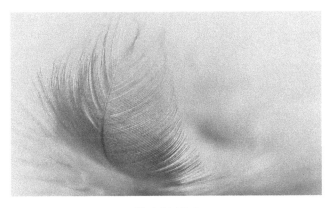

## – DAY 54 –

*"Our actions entrench the power of the light on this planet.*
*Every positive thought we pass between us makes room for more light."*
John Lewis

I choose love and light and positivity!
It may be daunting at times, yet I know positive thoughts affect the planet,
and even the universe, in magnificent ways.
A person who is grateful and believes in people's innate goodness,
and acts accordingly affects the world way more powerfully than those
who are dimly lit and have not yet awakened.

I believe this with all my heart
and it makes me even more thankful.

## – DAY 55 –

Thankful for the new, for transformation,
and for the possibilities that abound!

I am grateful for my willingness to push the envelope
of what has gone before in my life
I am so glad to be open to and listen to gentle whispers
by my higher self and the Divine within,
to decide on change where it is needed.

And then to go forward
with courage and commitment and joy.

## – DAY 56 –

As I progress on my spiritual path, I do my utmost not to judge.
What a challenge! I might think I know what is right or wrong, but
honestly, I know what is right and wrong for ME, and to have the audacity
to believe I know what is right for someone else is just incorrect.

A lot of the discord in the world has to do with people taking sides,
and seeing things without compromise; hating one another without
understanding or compassion.

I am very thankful to be accepting, to live and let live, and to know
I don't know as much as I want to believe I know.
I am grateful for the mystery of life, way vaster than our little minds
can fathom.

## – DAY 57 –

Today I am acknowledging the deep gratitude I have for creativity –
to the artists, authors and musicians who touch into Spirit
to express their gifts and talents; through colors, textures, musical notes
and word play in delightful and awe-inspiring ways.
And I toast creativity found in other areas of our lives too –
mathematicians, scientists, parents, inspirational speakers, teachers,
entrepreneurs – all are so creative too.

And most of all, I am thankful to the amazing creative urge of Mother
Nature that inspires me daily – seen in the spiral galaxies, exploding stars,
sacred ancient redwood trees, diverse flora, all creatures great and small,
and ever-changing rivers and deep, deep oceans.

CREATIVITY ABOUNDS!

## – DAY 58 –

*"I have the nerve to walk my own way, however hard, in my search for
reality, rather than climb upon the rattling wagon of wishful illusions."*
Zora Neale Hurston

I stand strong in my own quirkiness! I honor the part of me that is
determined and resolute, the part of me who loves me for exactly
who I am, and isn't swayed by popular opinion or media or hypnotized
group consciousness.

I am grateful that I don't jump on the bandwagon of consumerism or
competition or social climbing,
and instead appreciate in deep gratitude all that I have,
all that I am, and all whom I know.

*"The kind of beauty I want most is the hard-to-get kind that comes from within – strength, courage, dignity."*
Ruby Dee

I so appreciate beauty in every form, and showy Nature displays so much elegance, splendor and magnificence in her flowers, lush greenery and delightful assortment of creatures. I delight in the eye candy she presents each day.

And more than outer beauty, I am grateful for beauty within . . .
I am thankful for my own strength and bravery, for my own kindness and love expressed, for my integrity and honesty, including to myself.
The inner is so much more important than the outer
and I especially take time to remember that right now.

– D A Y  6 0 –

How grateful I am to be awake for the wake-up call!

Once I discovered what my purpose is during this unprecedented time,
I felt much more peaceful.
I believe each of us has a part in helping the world heal right now –
and that is to be kinder, to be purposely optimistic
despite gloom and doom reports, and to love more.

I know that it is so true that our thoughts create our reality
so I feel my job is to see what is right, see what is good, see what is
already healing.

Imagining a best-case scenario can only bring about the best!
Thankful to be aware and listening during this monumental time!

## – DAY 61 –

*"Our best chance to find the Oneness of Life is by looking with love into everything and everyone we meet.
Looking with love is a form of saying yes."*
Mark Nepo

I am so grateful to look with love upon all things.
I am glad to say YES to love, to good, to the beauty of life.
What we appreciate, appreciates
and expansive love is what I give and receive constantly.
I find, honestly, that my love quota is deepening and growing stronger
each and every day.
Indubitably thankful!

## – DAY 62 –

Today I give great thanks for our precious blue and green planet spinning in space. I give thanks for all precious creatures and all luscious fauna. What a wondrous world we live in!

I am conscious of the times I have not taken enough action toward helping to curb usage of fossil fuels (driving less); to lessen plastic use in my own home; and to heed scientists' warnings and do everything in my power to help, not hinder restoration.

My hope and prayer is that our modern oh-so-techy civilization slows down, and we can witness more and more rejuvenation happening around the world.

It is possible, and I am thankful that we can affect healing by our actions.

*"When we receive information, regardless of the source, our heart responds in various ways. It tells us whether or not we feel the vibration of truth in what we are hearing, seeing, and receiving. Our heart, intuition, and discernment work together to give us that feedback."*
Jonathan Goldman

How thankful I am for being able to listen to my heart.
I do know by my feelings if something rings true or not.
I do know when I meet someone if there is something "off" about their actions or honesty levels no matter what they say.
I have learned to trust my own heart, to trust my sacred intuition and neither lets me down.
So grateful to be able to tune into my higher self and the Universe's wisdom.

## – DAY 64 –

*"I allow myself to be authentic, especially when I feel that I am not enough."*
Rev. Sally Robbins

I appreciate self-honesty, which for me, has been learned.
I appreciate being what-you-see-is-what-you-get, not hiding "inappropriate" or down feelings.

It is so easy to pretend everything is okay and to deny uncomfortable feelings. How grateful I am to let others see the true me,
even if I'm not feeling completely confident, or even unworthy somehow.

What I know for sure is that I am worthy beyond measure, as we all are.
I am grateful for my authenticity and honesty, both inward and outward.

*"In the end, there are just three things that matter:*
*How well we have lived. How well we have loved.*
*How well we have learned to let go."*
Jack Kornfield

For me, the most challenging of these three things is to learn to let go.
And I know attachments keep me stuck.
How easy it is to be stuck on those I love dearly,
never wanting to lose them.
How easy it is to be stuck in my comfortable routines, with how I live.
I am very grateful to watch myself let go when it is needed.
I am very grateful to accept the things I cannot change, as the famous
Serenity Prayer goes. I am very grateful to live and love fiercely.

– DAY 66 –

I am grateful that I am not a hater, but a lover.

Understanding the Oneness of life, I know that if I hate, I hate myself.

I choose love in all instances, knowing that anyone who promotes hatred
or separation is just not understanding the Unity that exists, everywhere
and in everyone.

So thankful to realize we are all connected, and to act and speak
accordingly with gentleness, kindness, compassion,
and love.

I am grateful for my own sunny nature!
I tend to see the glass half full,
I enjoy wearing my rose-colored glasses,
and I am optimistic and cheery most of the time.
(Of course, I have my moods.)

I also so appreciate the upbeat people in my life who share these qualities.
How glad I am to have a bit of Pollyanna in me.

I am sure as can be that positive thoughts and feelings help the world!
Keep smiling . . .

– DAY 68 –

I am greatly thankful for
ACCEPTANCE.

It is the key to peace of mind; it is the key to letting go of my own agenda
when I really don't know what is right.

It is a way to garner patience if I think I know when something should
happen, and it doesn't.

To be spiritually mature, as I strive to be, I know that acceptance, allowing,
and surrender always help, they do not hinder.

I appreciate my ability to accept and surrender
to my Higher Power's wisdom.

*"In the stillness of the quiet, if we listen, we can hear the whisper of the heart giving strength to weakness, courage to fear, hope to despair."*
Howard Thurman

Silence is so sacred.
I gently welcome it in the morning, in the wee hours of dawn.
Every day I am thankful for this precious time to connect with Spirit,
with angelic presences, and with my own higher self.
The stillness offers replenishment, offers forgiveness, offers so much
that can't be seen or measured
but is the essence of life . . . love and peace and deep inner joy.
I am grateful to listen in the silence, and let that which is more
than me preside.

## – DAY 70 –

*"The head is like a public square. Anything at all can enter there, come,
cross over, go out, and create a lot of disorder . . .
It's not the head that has wings, it's the heart."*
Mirra Alfassa, known as The Mother

How grateful I am to listen to my compassionate, caring heart,
instead of letting that voice from my head worry and gnaw on crazy-
making thoughts, and fabricate scenarios as it tends to do.

I am deeply appreciative of the vital energy, the love and power,
the strength that is there when I hone in on my heart chakra.

When I go within and listen, true wisdom lives!
So very thankful.

*"Always hold fast to the present. Every situation, indeed every moment, is
of infinite value, for it is the representative of a whole eternity."*
Johann Wolfgang von Goethe

What a cosmic reminder this is.
I am grateful for all the benefits of staying in the now, which include
staying in peace, in plenty, in joy. And I love the idea of eternity held in the
present moment. Every tiny blade of grass, grain of sand, piece of earth,
molecule, atom and particle is a representative of all that is.

I relish my connection to the Oneness that is inherent in every single
person, place and thing – and I am both awestruck,
and supremely grateful.

There is a secret one inside us;
the planets in all the galaxies pass through his hands like beads,
That is a string of beads one should look at with luminous eyes.
Written by Kabir, 15th century Indian poet – translated by Robert Bly

– DAY 72 –

*"How do we look with spiritual eyes? Begin with kindness."*
David Ault

I am thankful to look at the world and its inhabitants with my spiritual eyes.

With that vision, everything and everyone is beautiful, is good,
is filled with light.

Judgment falls away . . . because I am positive that each person
is doing the absolute best they can.

I am supremely grateful for inner luminosity that helps me to see clearly
and kindly.

*"The more that we allow our hearts to expand to love, deeply appreciate, and feel inextricably tied to the places, things and people of this world, the more we are likely to take a stand on behalf of what we value."*
Kristi Nelson

It is sometimes tempting to close my heart – when someone hurts my feelings, when I feel rejection, when I lose someone precious to me. It is easy for me to lash out, to put up barriers, to decide I will close up. Yet as I grow more spiritually awake, I purposely keep my heart open in expansion, appreciating even the pain, feeling it and letting it go.

Love is the power that rules the universe and I am grateful to have an open, caring, loving heart. Today, I take a stand for love!

## – DAY 74 –

*"We are all multidimensional beings, crossing the dimensions at will and unknowingly. The higher your vibrations and natural positivity, the higher dimension you are dwelling upon."*
Andre Fau

I appreciate so very much knowing that the dimension we live in on a day-to-day basis is not the only one! As my consciousness expands, I can feel other dimensions even within myself, and when I am there, there is bliss, there is joy, there is deep peace.

There is so much more! Mystics from all ages report so too.
I am grateful for all the levels of existence, often invisible to us.
I am grateful for the veil between worlds lightening and lifting.

*"If you find yourself in a hole, stop digging."*
Will Rogers

These days, when I encounter obstacles, I don't push and shove to make things happen. I realize it is a sign from the Universe that a pause is needed and maybe I don't go forward with my plan after all.

Persistence is a virtue, and tenaciousness is sometimes a very good quality, but I know where my limits are, and don't get stuck in a hole of my own making.

I am so grateful to know when to listen to my inner guidance, and to let things go when it is right, resting in Divine right order and timing.

## – DAY 76 –

*"Wholeness is not a goal that we achieve. It's not a place that we can get to; it is an awareness that awakens within us."*
Sherri Mitchell

I am grateful for the harmonious wholeness and unity that is always there for me to tap into.

At my core is a serene, peaceful sense of completeness . . .
I can't always access it, yet I do touch into it when I am quiet,
when I go deep within, when I listen to inner guidance, when I realize how interconnected all of life is.

How glad I am to know that I am wholeness; I am well-being,
I am the perfection of God, with all of my qualities and shortcomings.

## – DAY 77 –

I am so thankful to realize that people and situations that may dismay me
are actually conjured up by me for my own growing and evolving!

As I can genuinely thank the person or event,
I move into a greater knowing
of my own power as an individualized expression of Spirit,
stemming from the Truth of who I am.

Thank you, Life, with all my heart,
for the learning and wisdom I am gaining (remembering)
in this lifetime.

## – DAY 78 –

*"Listen to the river sing sweet songs to rock my soul."*
Robert Hunter/Jerry Garcia

Oftentimes when I am down, I hear a tender voice within me that soothes
my cares and concerns.

It can happen when I've had a tough work day and I look around, and there is
so much still left to do – cleaning my messy house, making meals, walking our
dogs – just a few examples. I get tempted to feel overwhelmed.

The wise one within tells me "No worries, you will be fresh in the morning
and things will get done with grace and ease." I didn't always have this
support in my own mind, and it calms me down, and lets me give myself
a break. Great gratitude for the self-soothing I know how to do, and for
shiny, bright, brand new mornings!

ABUNDANCE IS EVIDENT IN EVERY NOOK AND CRANNY.

How grand it is to live in a universe with such infinite bounty . . .

I am grateful to live my life opening my arms wider and wider, to receive
all the good that is constantly offered to me.

I am thankful for the teeming life on this planet and beyond.
I feel humble when I ponder the diversity and grandeur
that has been created.

And I gratefully give of the plentiful gifts and love I offer.

– DAY 80 –

*"In this moment of quietude, this moment of devotion, this moment of
resolve, I let go of all that would inhibit my realization of my Oneness
with the Spirit."*
Michael B. Beckwith

I am grateful for the serenity of my heart and soul when I go within.
I am thankful for devoting time with absolute dedication to the Oneness
that I recognize in all of nature, in the zillions of stars each night,
in the clockwork of the seasons, and in all creatures great and small,
including humans.

This world is filled with judgment, divisiveness and separation, I realize.
And yet I know that if we could each consciously strive to feel the
connection of everything and everyone racial tensions would disappear,
love and peace would rule this world at last. Join me there.

## – DAY 81 –

In gratitude for my lifelong learning on a soul level,
to bring me where I am today.

How thankful I am to know, truly, that everything, absolutely everything,
happens for the evolution of our consciousness;
that I am shifting to a greater yet-to-be, and so is planet Earth
and its people, regardless of the evidence to the contrary.

Earth is a school and a world of contrasts.

Life can be heaven on Earth; let's make it so.

## – DAY 82 –

*"When we chase things, they can seem perpetually just out of reach.
There is an illusion of control in the chase. But the more we try to control,
the less control we actually have. When we let things go, what we are
searching for has the freedom to appear or even return to us."*
Emily Silva

How great it is to have learned life lessons that let me surrender more
easily. I know that there is Divine attraction, so that if I am meant to have
something or be with someone, I will be.
And no amount of coercion will help! In fact, it hinders.
Used to believe I could control the world. Ha!

I am grateful for acceptance and gentle acquiescence.

## – DAY 83 –

Thank you, Spirit, for sweet surprises.

Life goes along, at times mundane,
and then a "yes" from the universe slips in gently and lightly,
like a snowflake falling to the ground.

I love to be gifted with these surprises – they are usually not material
but a hint that I am on the right path, that my calling is worthwhile,
that I can affect the world as a benevolent light.

Deeply thankful.

## – DAY 84 –

Beauty abounds.
Love abounds.
Peace abounds.
Thank you, Spirit!

Grateful beyond measure when my vibration matches up
with beauty, love and peace.
It is always there, both inwardly and outwardly.

To allow my heart to open amplifies the exquisite beauty, the angelic love,
the serenity and soothing peace that exists for the taking.

This peace, love and beauty can prevail if we are open, if we are giving and
receiving in magnanimous, beneficial ways. And I am.

*"Do the best you can until you know better.*
*And when you know better, do better."*
Maya Angelou

I feel completely thankful to know every single person, yes, every single
man and woman, IS doing the best they can;
given their upbringing, given their social training
and given all their life experiences.
If you had known me 30 years ago, you would be so surprised.
I was out for myself; I over-imbibed and lived hedonistically.
And while I had a grand ol' time, mostly caring about me, myself and I,
how grateful I am to know better now, and to do better now.

– DAY 86 –

*"Not everything that can be faced can be changed, but nothing can be*
*changed that is not faced."*
James Baldwin

I know in my own life, I used to live in denial and hiding, especially to
myself! How could I see what needed to be changed if I wasn't willing to
be honest about my own problems?

I am extremely grateful that we as a society are looking at racism with
a magnifying glass right now; that so many are marching and keep
marching; that this matter seems not to be going away this time.
However, I feel encouraged that the scab and scourge of racial prejudice
has been picked. I am so thankful that we as a civilization are waking up
to what is wrong, lifting out of apathy, and I know this way the wrongs can
be remedied, at last.

*"The material world is but a fleeting shadow of the unseen."*
Myrtle Fillmore

Gratefully, I put stock in the unseen, which overrides and negates
all the seeming problems, evil and destruction of this world.
What is real is permanent, unchanging, and we can always go
to this realm in our minds.

The unseen that animates everything is creativity, is power, is love,
is the peace which passeth all understanding.

I am incredibly grateful to realize that what we can't see
with our human eyes is much more real than what we can see.

– DAY 88 –

*"When you can't go far, you go deep."*
Br. David Steindl-Rast

How grand it is to explore my own mind and heart and soul.
Each of us is a mini-cosmos, a microcosm of the Divine in human form.

I am grateful to be an inner explorer and navigator,
not dependent on outside travel.

I am thankful to know that everything is within me;
we are deep and vast like infinity
with layers and layers to explore.

*"Everything is built in your favor, Dear One, and we await your decision to stand in the light of this joy."*
Doreen Virtue

I know and believe that angels cheer us on;
that the Divine supports and protects us;
that life is basically Good despite big and little challenges;
that we can bask in the glory of love and light and peace and joy
at any chosen moment.

How supremely grateful I am to consistently feel guidance and angelic presence and God's love.

– DAY 90 –

*"For many years, at great cost, I traveled through many countries, saw the high mountains, the oceans. The only things I did not see were the sparkling dewdrops in the grass just outside my door."*
Rabindranath Tagore

I am incredibly grateful to pay attention to all the tiny and vast miracles that are literally right outside my doorstep.

Nature constantly reveals the blessing of life, the beauty of life,
the joy of life.

I stop and breathe, I live in the present moment, and when I do,
sparkling wonders do await.

*"Every day we are engaged in a miracle which we don't even recognize: a
blue sky, white clouds, green leaves, the black,
curious eyes of a child – our own two eyes. All is a miracle."*
Thich Nhat Hanh

So thankful to be present to the miracles that abound.
I wake up with a thank you in my heart and as the day begins, often there
is this wondrous golden light shining in the early morning time.

I say thank you for my eyes that see, for the love all around me and within
me, for the peace and splendor of every single day.
LIFE IS SO GOOD and I am filled with appreciation from sunrise
to deep, starry nights.

– DAY 92 –

*"Gratitude places you in the energy field of plentitude. Glow with gratitude
and see how awe and joy will make their home in you."*
Michael B. Beckwith

I am grateful to be filled with appreciation for all that is.

I am grateful to be glowing with gratitude.

I am grateful to live in plentitude of all good . . . friends, family, love,
peace, prosperity and vibrant health.
I am grateful to welcome awe and joy to live with me.

Thank you, abundant overflowing universe!

## – DAY 93 –

*"With freedom, books, flowers and the moon,*
*who could not be happy?"*
Oscar Wilde

Fill in your own list of your very favorite things.

Mine include yes, freedom, books, flowers and the moon,
and also trees and rivers and lakes and seas.
Loving people, all the creatures of this Earth, aurora borealis, the zillions of
stars in the night sky, sunshine and clouds . . .
and all the invisible yet very real qualities of life such as peace,
joy, bliss, abundance and harmony.

With all of this and so much more, how could I not be happy?

## – DAY 94 –

*"The path is easy for those who have no preferences."*
Sanaya Roman

While I know it is good to have some preferences, otherwise I get
"whatever," being fixated on preferences or expectations exactly how I
want them just does not serve me.

If I am attached to the outcome I want, and I'm not getting it, I get upset
or angry or frustrated. Far better to know that there is a bigger picture;
that a Higher Power is guiding us, and let myself just accept that what I
want is not happening (yet) in this situation.

When I can truly let go of my preferences, I am grateful to allow peace to
reign in my heart and soul, no matter the outside circumstances.

## – DAY 95 –

*"He who is contented is rich."*
Lao Tzu

I know that I am rich beyond measure because I am satisfied
with all that I have and am and do. I am rich in love, peace and joy.

This definitely goes against society's beliefs, which measure prosperity
with money, status and possessions.

I am so thankful to be predominately happy, and to realize my life
is truly filled with plenty!

## – DAY 96 –

*"Deep beneath the random and shifting waves of my mind,
I discover a vast ocean of peace."*
Unity Daily Word, March 5, 2016

So thankful to be able to find that ocean of peace within me . . .
to have the ability to get quiet,
to let the hustle and bustle of my overactive mind slow down
and to sink into the solace of peaceful calm.

In the silence, I find comfort,
no matter what kind of raucousness goes on in the outside world.

## – DAY 97 –

*"Swim in the ocean of vastness and peace and limitless happiness*
*beyond dreams – within yourself."*
Paramahansa Yogananda

It's there within me! I feel and know it.
The infinity of joy and serenity does reside inside me,
within my soul and spirit.
I take solace and comfort in that vast ocean of good,
whenever outer circumstances tell me differently.

Thank you, God, for all of the magnificence you have instilled
into each of your creations, including me.

## – DAY 98 –

*"It is not a question of whether you 'have what it takes,' but of whether*
*you take the gifts you have – they are plenteous – and share them*
*with all the world."*
Neale Donald Walsch

The profuse gifts bestowed by the universe are so incredibly lavish.
I marvel every single day at all I am given by birthright.

In the awareness that I actually do have all that it takes,
I gladly share my bountiful gifts with the world –
presents of gratitude, of love, of peace within, of optimism,
of creativity, of beauty and of well-being.

And what I give freely comes back to me tenfold. What a deal!

## – DAY 99 –

*"You are not here to change anyone. You are here to shift your own
perception to see things rightly, not to set things rightly."*
Michael B. Beckwith

What a relief to know I'm not in charge of shifting anyone or anything else
but myself. I try sometimes, and it is always futile, and leads to frustration.

It is enough of a challenge for me to see things rightly,
let alone trying to put the world in order!

When I know I'm in charge of me and nobody else,
I am filled with serenity, peace, calm and a sense that all is well in my world.
And the good feelings I muster help rather than hinder.
Filled with gratitude for self-reflection so I can be the very best me I can be.

## – DAY 100 –

*"How can you follow the course of your life
if you do not let it flow?"*
Lao Tzu

Acceptance of what is allows flow.
How glad I am to accept, to allow, to let my expectations fall away
and let go.

This is definitely not always easy, I can be tenacious, and want and expect
things to go a certain way.
I can be dogged in trying to make life go the way I want it to go.

Yet, when I can relax and flow with what is and what is not,
I let my life takes its natural, Divine course.

## – DAY 101 –

*"No matter how difficult the day, there's always something
to be grateful for."*
Laura Markham, PhD

I've got to admit sometimes I have a crabby out-of-sorts day.
Today is one of those!
However, as I write this gratitude to you, I am positive my mood will be
uplifted because that is what being grateful brings.
It is guaranteed.

So the next time you feel mad or upset,
summon up the things you feel most grateful for.

## – DAY 102 –

How glad I am for blossoming, bountiful spring!

The new growth of this season is expectant with promise.
My heart is glad for the coming of more light, more warmth
and the bright, lush green of springtime.

The birds start a'singing, and the frogs start croaking their glorious chorus
each night.

My heart blooms in joy and hope and expectation
like the profusion of all the newness of nature
this time of year.

## – DAY 103 –

I can be (and mostly keep it to myself) envious, jealous,
and compare myself unfavorably to others.

I am grateful to be in the process of giving this craziness up!

The truth is, I am amazing and splendid precisely as I am (as you are, and
as each person is with all the potential that is God-given).

I consciously fill myself up with self-love and positive noncompetitive
thoughts, instead of the opposite which just doesn't serve me.

How thankful I am to use all the tools in my spiritual toolbox to allow
myself to change my mind.

## – DAY 104 –

Peace begins with me.

I absolutely love how empowered I truly am.

No matter what happens in the material world, my peace begins with me.

I am grateful to give up griping; to let myself forgive; to realize every
person does the very best they can from where they are;
and deep peace is always lodged in my heart, in my soul,
in my entire being.

All I have to do is breathe and relax, and ah! there it is.

Grateful!

*"To love life truly is to be whole in all one's parts;
and to be whole in all one's parts is to be free and unafraid."*
Howard Thurman

How grateful I am to know I am whole and complete exactly as I am.
Having a partner is very nice, but I know I have everything I need within
myself and knowing this, I am unfettered and strong.

The secret for me is knowing I am never alone; that a greater power or
God is within me and always watching out for me,
and that is true freedom!

So thankful.

– D A Y 1 0 6 –

*"Appreciation is the vessel for future blessings."*
Michael Berg

Such a simple message and so profound!
What you appreciate, appreciates!

If I am feeling down and I write what I'm grateful for,
my mood magically uplifts.

With appreciation, I know the secret to expanding more and more good
in my life
and I'm so very grateful.

*"Whatever our souls are made of, yours and mine are the same."*
Emily Bronte

We are so much more the same than different.

I am thankful to feel the Oneness of humankind that is always there.

My soul, which is just like your soul, loves and appreciates
our commonalities.

## – DAY 108 –

*"Current models of our cells' biology
tells us that every thought and experience we have is
transmitted immediately to the cells in our body."*
Ruth Miller

So extremely thankful to know to be vigilant with my thoughts, to live as
much as I can in a positive vibration, to realize that how I respond to my
experiences is absolutely essential for my body's well-being.

I rise up in joy! I rise up in peace!
I shift to what I do want rather than lingering on what I don't.

This is a simple philosophy to state that is not always so easy to live.
I am committed to it though, and am in deep gratitude for the power
I possess to make this happen.

*"To see a World in a Grain of Sand
And a Heaven in a Wild Flower
Hold Infinity in the palm of your hand
And Eternity in an hour."*
William Blake

Thankful for turning a fixed viewpoint upside down, and seeing it in a
whole new way – like an abstract painting that can be rotated,
and each vista is amazing. To look, really look at a blossom close up,
studying it, and all of a sudden it is much more than I've ever seen before;
a tiny cosmos in its own right.

Life IS dazzling and filled with grand surprises
and I am ever grateful.

– DAY 110 –

*"The grace of a river is a reminder of how nature seeks elegance and
achieves immense beauty of cohesion and balance . . .
if only our lives could achieve, or indeed allow, such grace and elegance."*
John O'Donohue

I am grateful for the steady flow of meandering nearby rivers!

I have a passionate love affair with rivers, and it is pure joy to swim in
them on hot summer days.

Yet I am even more thankful for the flow in my life.
If I relax and let myself float along, trusting I am being guided, instead of
pushing or struggling, all is grace and ease.
How happy I am when I can let go!

## – DAY 111 –

Thankful to be loving, to be loved, and to be in love with life.

I believe that one definition of God IS love, and that when all is said
and done, how we have loved others and ourselves
is the most important aspect of life.

Certainly it is not all the stuff we own, or status symbols we collect!

I am grateful to worship at the altar of love, sweet love!

## – DAY 112 –

*"Attention is the rarest and purest form of generosity."*
Simone Weil

I feel deep gratitude for magnanimous souls,
evidenced in so many ways, bountifully.

People demonstrate their generous ways with attention, listening and
giving of time; in kind acts, in paying it forward, in unconditional loving.

When someone understands the abundance of life then they can give
freely of their gifts because they know they won't run out!

It feels so satisfying to be generous, with no strings attached,
and I strive to be that always.

*"An emotion comes, stays for a while, and goes away, just like a storm.
If you're aware of that, you won't be afraid of your emotions."*
Thich Nhat Hanh

I am so grateful to be tapped into peace and solace and calm at my core.

I am thankful to count on the fluctuation of all my emotions;
to acknowledge them and let them come out in full force, truly
feeling them and then eventually to watch them float away.

This too shall pass.
Amen.

– DAY 1 1 4 –

I am grateful for the occasional disagreement
with trusted, evolved friends.

I am thankful for the people I know who speak their truth and don't
hold back, and who listen in return.

This allows more understanding and harmony, if not immediately,
then eventually.

And when we talk it out, much is learned.

It takes bravery, courage and trust, mixed with love to air things out.

And I appreciate those qualities in me and my friends.

*"Trees are everything I long to be: deep, tall, gorgeous, hospitable, and un-apologetically assertive as they stretch upward in hungry yearning for the sky."*
Patricia Adams Farmer

Trees have no need to chatter, they demonstrate the loveliness of cherished silence. When I am underneath the umbrella of ancient redwoods, the din of activity ceases in my own heart and soul.
The hush is palpable and deeply renewing.

Each tree is unique, and I really doubt that they compare or compete like we do. They house the ferns, the mushrooms, the rhododendrons and all the forest creatures. They help us breathe! They support so much life. I am deeply thankful for our symbiotic relationship with the forests, and also the trees that brighten up cities and neighborhoods with their shaded beauty.

## – DAY 116 –

I am thankful, so thankful, for the power of imagination.

When I begin imagining something new,
I invoke the magic of creation!

As I strengthen my vision, it begins to come true!

The infinite Creator has given us so much –
and today I appreciate
the dreaming power of my mind.

*"Working on our own consciousness is the most important thing that we are doing at any moment, and being love is the supreme creative act."*
Ram Dass

How thankful I am to have learned I can only change my own mind and heart, and that is enough to do indeed!

With my own small steps to expand my wisdom and knowledge about what I believe, I benefit all.

And I am so grateful to be a love artist, painting my world with caring, compassion and nurturing!

– DAY 118 –

I am so appreciative of the growing confidence in myself.
This goes hand in hand with fostering self-love and appreciation.

It is a humble confidence, that has been nurtured as I remember that Spirit is within me, as well as all around me. I realize that I am supported by the whole wide universe!

I am filled with energy, creativity, zeal and excitement for what comes next.

*"Yet to love someone is an art.*
*It does not come simply or cheaply but is a lifetime's work."*
John O'Donohue

I am grateful for my own loving, caring, nurturing, supportive nature.
I have honed it through the years so that I am no longer codependent,
yet I still watch over my loved ones, and it does take experience, patience
and wisdom to love deeply. It is perhaps most difficult for me to love
myself. On the surface I do, but sometimes feeling compassion for myself
is tricky. I am thankful to grow in self-love, loving myself and others in a
healthy, unconditional way, in a giving no-strings-attached way.
And I know loving and being open to be loved is our most important work,
and stretches over lifetimes.

– DAY 120 –

*"I believe that the greatest truths of the universe don't lie outside, in the*
*study of the stars and the planets. They lie deep within us,*
*in the magnificence of our heart, mind, and soul."*
Anita Moorjani

I deeply appreciate all the reminders, like this one, that I receive
that the answers lie within me.
That each of us is a brilliant, creative, loving manifestation of Spirit,
in microcosm.

To truly know and feel this leads me to profound peace,
to being the love essence that I truly am.
And in this vibration, I am absolutely sure that ALL IS WELL.
Thank you.

## – DAY 121 –

Sometimes I am challenged by things gone awry – it can be almost
comical when my computer is obviously playing tricks on me
if it wasn't so darn aggravating.

Today was a day like this.

And what I can find to be grateful for is that every day is a fresh new start,
and that my tomorrow will be undoubtedly much more joyful and easy
after a day filled with quite the opposite of Divine Right Order.

I am grateful for the preponderance of grace, ease and glory that is my life!

## – DAY 122 –

Today, I am incredibly grateful for the antidotes that exist to the main TV
media news, which can be so very negative and depressing.
I look at an app called Good News Network on my phone to cheer me up.

Here is a sample of the first few headlines from today's true stories:
• MIT researchers believe they've developed a new treatment for easing
the passage of kidney stones.
• After reading random Facebook posts, hikers retrieve lost wedding ring
from snowy mountain trail.
• These vegan, edible and long-lasting wheat bowls are cutting down on
plastic tableware.

People, I truly believe there IS so much good, positive stuff happening
every single day. And I am thankful to focus on the good, and to turn off
the negativity, and that includes in my own mind too!

*"If you are willing to look at another person's behavior toward you
as a reflection of the state of their relationship with themselves
rather than a statement about your value as a person,
then you will, over a period of time, cease to react at all."*
Yogi Bhajan

I am grateful to realize that I am worthy, I am worthy, I AM worthy!

My self-esteem stems from within, it does not come from any person
or exterior condition.

So, I am thankful to count on my own self-love to carry the day.

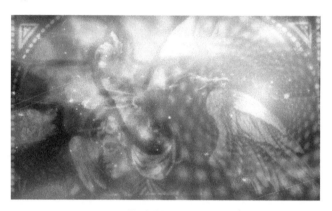

## – DAY 124 –

*"Giving frees us from the familiar territory of our own needs by opening our
mind to the unexplained worlds occupied by the needs of others."*
Barbara Bush

Giving is truly receiving – we get love and joy back into our own hearts even
if we are anonymous in our giving. It's feel amazing to freely give and share!

I knew a minister once who taught me that if I'm depressed, the best way
to get out of my funk is to think about what I can give, and then to give it!
It sounds unlikely to find that sharing instead of moping turns our mood
around. But it has proved to be very invaluable advice. It works.

There are great ways to give monetarily, and don't forget powerful prayers
and sending healing love energy.

*"Gratitude is so close to the bone of life, pure and true, that it instantly stops the rational mind, and all its planning and plotting."*
Regina Sara Ryan

Along with all the other proven benefits to being grateful – better health, more joy, more peace, greater well-being (which are proven in scientific studies), how grand to know that gratitude is a tool to turn off all those distracting, crazy thoughts that deter us from the here and now.

If I am tossing and turning in the middle of the night,
I let my mind tackle instead all that I am grateful for
and yes, I find that I can relax and rest.
So thankful for the power of gratefulness.

– DAY 126 –

*"When before the beauty of a sunset or a mountain, you pause and exclaim, 'Ah,' you are participating in Divinity."*
Ancient Hindu Text

Nature is glorious! Nature is restorative! Nature calms me down.

I honor and worship the beauty of nature, in all its flamboyance and diverse expressions.

Thank you, Spirit, for the Creation of Life.

For sunsets and mountains and the wisdom of trees.

I am so grateful. Ahhh . . .

*"If I could, I'd hold my fear and baptize it in the lake of my heart."*
Mark Nepo

I am thankful for the idea of love baptizing fear!

Fear stands in the way of going forward, of healing and forgiving.

I wash my fear in love and let it subside, gently.

Deeply grateful.

– DAY 128 –

*"Laughter is carbonated holiness."*
Anne Lamott

I appreciate so much those who don't take life so darn seriously,
as I can tend to sometimes.
I love laughter! I love silliness! I love the people in my life, including my
hubby, who easily find the humor, and make me laugh uproariously.
One of my favorite things in life is to enjoy deep belly laughs,
the kind where my stomach starts hurting I am laughing so hard.

Thank you, wonderful Anne,
for reminding me that laughter is a form of holiness.

## – DAY 129 –

*"When your dreams turn to dust, vacuum."*
Wolfgang Riebe

I am thankful for this witty and wise advice.

Fighting to make something happen can often mean it is not to be.
I notice and heed the blockages when they arise.

And then, I release the dream, take a deep breath, tidying up
the shattered pieces, making way for ever bigger
and more wondrous dreams!

## – DAY 130 –

Thinking of my earlier life before I found out how potent gratitude is,
I was kind of a spoiled complainer!
And I had absolutely nothing to gripe about! (just like now)

How grand it is to celebrate all that is good and right, focusing on the
abundance of blessings that are always here.

How grand it is to be an optimistic dreamer, even in such a crazy world.

How simple, yet sometimes challenging it is, to stay in the vibration
of gratefulness

I am ever-thankful to know of this powerful practice and to stay steady on
the path, no matter what.

*"We have been given this precious human incarnation in which each and every one of us is a candidate for enlightenment."*
Michael B. Beckwith

I daresay we are candidates for enlightenment even if we kick and scream and do our best not to wake up!

How grateful I am to live in a conscious way, inviting in learning and growing and most of all, remembering.

My cozy routines and comfort zone often get knocked out of balance, and it makes me proud that I can flow with disruption and even upheaval. I couldn't be more thankful for my ability to transform and let go.

## – DAY 132 –

*"Being in love means seeing the Beloved all around me."*
Ram Dass

So thankful for my openness and willingness to love . . . to love me . . . to love you . . . to love all.

I truly love every aspect of the Beloved, which includes all people, all creatures, all nature, the microcosms of life that are in every inch of ground on this planet and the Infinite Universe – the galaxies, stars, planets and life in other realms we cannot see.

I love purely and I love deeply. This is not to say I fall out of love sometimes. I am human. But I have the greatest gratitude I can find in my heart for loving and loving more.

*"If you realized how powerful your thoughts are,*
*you would never think a negative thought."*
Peace Pilgrim

I celebrate the positivity and optimism
in my heart and soul, which comes so naturally
especially when I remember to be grateful,
during good times or bad.

Thank you, Life.

– DAY 134 –

*"Whenever I experience something beautiful, I am with Soul.*
*That moment of inward breath, that pause and awareness of*
*'how beautiful this is' is a prayer of appreciation,*
*a moment of gratitude in which I behold beauty and am one with it."*
Jean Shinoda Bolen

I am thankful for the awe of beauty, the "ahhhh" of beauty.
Every single day there is something so beautiful to admire,
often from Mother Nature; and sometimes in the lovely smile and eyes of
an open, caring person.

We are graced with beauty! It is always there for the beholding.

And I am so grateful to feel it, know it and savor it each and every day.

*"Trust yourself. Create the kind of self that you will be happy to live with all your life."*
Golda Meir

So pleased to know and trust myself, absolutely sure that my intentions are pure even when I take a misstep.

I love me for me, quirkiness and sterling qualities, one and all.

And with this love, I expand it, and love all of the world's inhabitants!

I am deeply thankful to feel true self-love so that I lead a joyful, creative and fulfilling life.

# – DAY 136 –

*"Be a true representative of the goodness in your heart, and don't expect it to be easy or even noticed."*
Adyashanti

I am grateful to be kind; to pay it forward, not expecting anything in return. The payback is in my own heart and soul,
when I know I have been the best Deborah I can be.

Kindness for kindness' sake!

May the world be transformed with more lovingkindness and peace, and may it start with each one of us.

## – DAY 137 –

*"No one saves us but ourselves.*
*No one can and no one may.*
*We ourselves walk the path."*
Buddha

How grateful I am to realize that I am the only person in charge of me.
Nothing outside myself can save me nor destroy me.
That means that I am free.

How good it is to know I have freedom of actions, feelings,
and how I perceive the outside world.
I am thankful!

## – DAY 138 –

*"What we have once enjoyed, we can never lose.*
*All that we love deeply becomes a part of us."*
Helen Keller

So very sad to lose a person or pet that we love.
Yet, love lives on and never ever dies.
How marvelous is that?!

My mother died 30 years ago, and I love her as much today as I ever did.

I can't imagine losing a precious sister or my husband or any dear friend
yet that will happen in life and I am grateful that love burns brightly like
a candle flame, and cannot be extinguished. And I believe we will meet
again on the other side.

*"For it is in giving that we receive."*
Francis of Assisi

I am grateful to truly understand that what I give away comes back to me tenfold and that more important, when I give freely with no strings attached, it makes me feel enriched and oh-so-abundant.

When I'm feeling depleted or experiencing lack, I know that the best thing I can do for myself is to give love, creativity and gifts of all kinds to others.

So, I'm very thankful for the principle of Divine circulation, which is a stream of good flowing everywhere all the time.

## – DAY 140 –

*"Joy is what happens to us when we allow ourselves
to recognize how good things really are."*
Marianne Williamson

Gosh, gratitude always sounds so very simple, and it truly is.

Sometimes, though, remembering can be the challenge.

I am thankful to focus on the good, focus on what is right,
focus on what's beautiful in life,
and feel my joy levels bubble up and rise!

*"Every step forward is worth one hundred steps back.
That is the nature of the learning process. Every time you embrace truth,
years of false beliefs are released."*
Paul Ferrini

Tonight I give great thanks for spiritual and emotional evolution.
It does sometimes feel that I have taken too many steps back,
but in learning, it is true that we are always ahead of where we started.

Like riding a bike, we won't forget once we embark upon a new adventure.

I am SO grateful to be on a track that leads me to greater understanding
and wisdom, not only about myself, but helps me more fully comprehend
the world and others.

– DAY 142 –

*"So much has been given to me; I have no time to ponder
over that which has been denied."*
Helen Keller

I am in absolute gratitude for the gift of life:
for all the people, nature and blessings that make my life precious.
I focus on what is gifted to me, and it so much!

And I give great thanks for all that I am, all that I have, all whom I love
and for the beauty, splendor and magic of life.
I have absolutely everything I need, always.

Thank you, God–Goddess–All-That-Is!

*"Look inside. The way lies dancing to the melodies spun out
by your own heart. This is a symphony. All the rest are jingles."*
Anna Quindlen

Let me dance to the rhythms of my own heart and soul,
where wisdom abides, where joy bubbles up from the reeds and violins
and percussion.

I absolutely recognize that nobody knows better than me what is best for
me. I honor, respect and appreciate the harmonious symphony always
playing within if I stop and listen.
The conductor is Spirit or God or the Higher Power within.
Deeply thankful.

## – DAY 144 –

*"What can we gain by sailing to the moon if we are not able
to cross the abyss that separates us from ourselves?
This is the most important of all voyages of discovery."*
Thomas Merton

I am filled with great gratitude to be on a path of self-discovery; knowing
myself better than any other time before. If I feel separate, from myself
or others, I know that I am in reality fooling myself. After all, I couldn't be
separate from the Oneness that is everywhere present if I tried.
And my egoic self definitely tries!

My sail is set to voyage toward better self-understanding, toward more
self-love, toward inner peace.
And when I get there, I share my peace and love with the world!

## – DAY 145 –

*"When the roots are deep, there is no reason to fear the wind."*
Chinese Proverb

My roots are strong in faith. I ground myself in trust,
transcending all the human pains and glory
that do always pass like the wind.

I am grateful, that like a mighty tree,
I can silently rest in the wisdom of the ages,
filled with serenity, profound love and joy.

## – DAY 146 –

I am incredibly grateful for all of the things and people in life
that bring me JOY!

Today, I celebrate art, glorious art! I am thankful to create
for no logical reason except to create.

Using my right-brain intuition and discovery;
simply enjoying the process, putting marks on paper,
watching what becomes visible, one just never knows . . .
is SO freeing, so relaxing, and fills my heart with joy and fulfillment.

Thank you, Great Creator, for the art that is everywhere – in reflections,
sunsets and sunrises, rainbows, flowers, zebras with their stripes and
multicolored toucans –
and while I'm thanking you, thank you for my own ability to create!

## – DAY 147 –

*"If you're the same person at fifty that you were at twenty,
you've wasted thirty years."*
Muhammad Ali

My path has been such a meandering path, from the straight-and-narrow
workaday world, to decadent slips in my integrity and maturity,
to full-on spiritual growth.

Yes, I have learned a LOT in 30+ years! I am a better, kinder, more
unselfish person, most definitely. And I am very grateful for that.

I'm also grateful for my life exactly as it has been, since my wayward path
has gifted me with more empathy and compassion for others.

## – DAY 148 –

*"I look up at the blue sky and the bare chestnut tree, on whose branches little
raindrops shine, appearing like silver, and at the seagulls and other birds as
they glide on the wind. As long as this exists . . . and I may live to see it,
this sunshine, these cloudless skies, while this lasts I cannot be unhappy."*
Anne Frank

This passage reminds me of how very much I have to be grateful for.

I am deeply thankful for the miracles and magic of life itself; a surprise
deep blue sky in the midst of winter, looking up at awe-inspiring
multitudes of stars in a clear night sky.

And I am incredibly thankful for all the comfort and safety of the peaceful
home where I reside.
If Anne Frank could be so grateful, certainly so can I!

*"It is only with the heart that one can see rightly;
what is essential is invisible to the eye."*
Antoine de Saint-Exupery

I am grateful to notice what my heart tells me and how it responds;
I can trust my heart and intuition so much more than my logical mind as
my brain often caters to my ego, whereas my heart never does.

Seeing the world through love is the only answer. The people who inflict
pain and suffering just don't understand that we are all connected so by
hurting others they cannot be immune to the pain.

What is essential is love, joy, peace, wisdom and all the other invisible
attributes of Spirit. I am so thankful to see with my heart.

– DAY 150 –

*"The more that we allow our hearts to expand to love, deeply appreciate,
and feel inextricably tied to the places, things and people of this world, the
more we are likely to take a stand on behalf of what we value."*
Kristi Nelson

I am so glad to continually expand my heart into more love
and more appreciation.

It feels SO good and in contrast, it feels so bad to be in a state of hatred,
dislike or feeling ungrateful. Ugh!

The more I exponentially expand my gratitude, the more it becomes a
healthy habit, and I find I do feel more connected to every living part of
this world, and beyond. I am grateful to stand strong for what I believe.

I am thankful to be a renegade when I need to be.
Sometimes I must take a stand, and do what I believe is right, even when
it's not popular, even when hardly anyone I know agrees.

Several times I needed to speak my truth publicly, and once at the Center
where I worship, I stood up and said what I needed to say, and watched one
spiritual friend roll her eyes, as so many others disagreed with my points.
When the vote was taken, I "lost" but kept my own integrity speaking up!

When I stay true to my beliefs, they can go against the grain of mainstream
society. I do weigh the facts, but I also lean heavily on my own intuition,
which always leads me in the right direction. I am grateful to be a maverick,
standing strong in my own power, fueled by Spirit within.

– DAY 152 –

*"Your soul is a compass. Change one coordinate in your spiritual compass
and you change your entire life's direction."*
Caroline Myss

I listen and pay heed to the direction my soul wishes to go.

My inner compass has changed the course of my life in dramatic ways,
toward spiritual fulfillment and joy and purpose.
Listening to the still, small voice within is paramount.

I am so thankful for Divine guidance.

*"Whatever is within the flowers is within us. We are a part of this universe!*
*Whether I'm looking at a human hand or looking at the galaxies of shooting*
*stars or the flight of a bird . . . something marvelous is going on and I'm*
*part of it. We're all part of it!"*
Harold Feinstein

There is so much commonality between us. There is so much to
appreciate in each person, no matter political views or divergent
upbringing. We are way, way more alike than we are different.
And this extends to the commonality between all living things.
And it thrills me to no end to realize everything in the universe is alive.
I am grateful to focus on what we have in common
and feel harmony, feel peace, feel serenity and feel deep love for all.

– DAY 154 –

*"The soul often speaks through longing."*
Sue Monk Kidd

My soul wants to evolve, by letting go of hindrances to the love and
wisdom that I am deep within.
Sometimes I feel restless, and I can feel a sea change coming.

It happened dramatically at the ending of my first marriage –
in fact, I moved geographically to a new state, and my whole life
was upended (in a positive way).

I dearly love my routines and daily life, but I also love exploring uncharted
territory. So, I am grateful to listen to my soul and quench its longing
when I can.

*"Yes!*
*I meet life with a resounding yes today!"*
Unity Daily Word, February 19, 2017

I am thankful for my tendency to say yes, rather than no.
Sure, I have boundaries and sometimes a clear "no" is needed
but part of the joy in life is the unknown, the mystery, the vast field
of possibilities that we can explore.

I say yes to life, and life says yes to me!
Infinitely grateful.

– DAY 156 –

I am so thankful for benevolence.
I find an act of kindness, a gift of any kind, sweetness, a propensity for
good to all be beautiful benevolence.

I do feel with all my heart that the universe is benevolent,
that people are almost always kind and loving and helpful,
unless life has thwarted their innate goodness, which happens, of course.

I am grateful for the supportive power that is within and through
everything which I call God.

And I am grateful for my own giving, loving, benevolent heart.
Thank you.

*"A bird is safe in its nest –*
*but that is not what its wings are made for."*
Amit Ray

I am so thankful to stretch my wings and fly!
It is easier to stay in my comfort-zone nest, secure and cozy,
yet I believe life is for growing and learning and adapting and shifting
and trying out new things, unafraid.
I am deeply grateful for the grand adventure of life.

*"Problems dissolve in expanded awareness.*
*As our consciousness expands, a solution emerges."*
Michael B. Beckwith

I am grateful to realize I can always trust the Divine within me to help me
solve problems that present themselves.
Sometimes, I feel confused and unsure how to resolve issues in my life
and then I breathe deeply and relax, trusting in guidance I can always
count on. I go within in my prayer and meditation time to listen to
God–Goddess–All-That-Is and my highest self.
Sometimes I go to bed asking for a solution, and it comes.

My evolving, growing consciousness helps me navigate troubles and strife,
absolutely. How thankful am I.

## – DAY 159 –

Today I turn away from worry, fear and doubt.

They do not serve me, and I let them go.

Instead I focus on the magical, mystical qualities of life
that are the true reality.

I put my trust and faith in the Good.

I appreciate the love, abundance, peace and joy of Spirit –
and all of it expands!

## – DAY 160 –

*"The least movement is of importance to all nature. The entire ocean is
affected by a pebble."*
Blaise Pascal

If I really know this, then I will be more attentive to my every move –
physically, emotionally and spiritually.

It is so important to be kind, to walk gently on the Earth;
to refrain from blurting out angry, venomous words; to hold compassion
in my heart, and not try to numb myself from suffering and injustices.

I know that everything is inextricably linked, and one small act of
sweetness, one appreciated heartfelt compliment, one loving-kindness
ripples out and helps heal the world.

## – DAY 161 –

*"Habit is habit and not to be flung out of the window*
*by any man, but coaxed downstairs a step at a time."*
Mark Twain

I am a creature of habit, I like my routines awfully well.
It is a challenge but oh-so-worthwhile to let go of habits not serving me.

I am grateful for the idea of being patient with myself when an unwanted
practice persists.
I have tendencies to be impulsive and rash
and that isn't really in harmony with the part of me
that wants to fight change.
So I am thankful for gentle nudging and persistence.

## – DAY 162 –

*"As you become enlightened, as you release the obstacles, the hindrances,*
*the limitations, the interpretations of the past, you wake up to your intrinsic*
*nature, you wake up to sanity."*
Michael B. Beckwith

Glad I am to let go of past blocks and wake up to my intrinsic nature –
which is love, which is beauty, which is creativity, which is peace.
No longer addicted to being what society pushes me to be,
I am free, I am liberated, I am devoted to my unique calling.
I am grateful to be a gratitude aficionado and to share it with the world.

And as Rickie Byars proclaims in her beautiful song
"I am free in the Spirit. Yes I'm only here for God."

*"Heartbreak and hope are not mutually exclusive. We can be angry and sad and filled with longing for something we cannot have, and simultaneously we can be grateful for what we've got – aware, for reasons we'd never choose, of what really matters and what doesn't."*
Lennon Flowers

How glad I am to know that things are not simply black or white. Life is so complicated, with many shades of gray. On the spectrum of emotions, I can simultaneously feel grief, along with a glimmer of joy. Emotions are a vast arena, and none should be ignored. If I'm sad or heartbroken or filled with grief, I sit with those feelings. I don't deny them. I am grateful not to try to spiritually bypass sorrow or anger.

I am grateful we are so multifaceted and resilient as spiritual human beings.

## – DAY 164 –

*"Prayer is not a religious activity. It is a soul power, a cosmic force. It is the intimate sacred language of the celestial realm that unites us all."*
Caroline Myss

Prayer is so sacred indeed. I engage in prayer daily, and when I do,
I speak to the All-in-All,
the omnipresent, omniactive, omniscient universal wisdom.

For me, there is no man in the sky, judging and wielding power over us.
So I do not beseech or beg, I pray my intentions for good.

I believe God is love, and love is everywhere and within everything.
And I am SO incredibly grateful for this, the glue that connects us all.

## – DAY 165 –

Today I am grateful for a resolute reset!

Slipping sometimes into lifelong patterns of worry and fear,
I catch myself, and gently remind myself that I have let those habits go!

One of my strengths is tenacity
So today, right now, I am tenaciously tending to trust and faith,
feeling my vibration rise . . .
knowing all is well, and I am always, always, always supported
and guided, every day, every step of the way.

## – DAY 166 –

*"A good deed doesn't just evaporate and disappear.
Its consequences saturate the universe and the goodness that happens
somewhere, anywhere, helps in the transfiguration of the ugliness."*
Desmond Tutu

This is good news, as I am aware that there are so many good deeds done
by good people every single day.

It helps, exponentially, in the transforming of the world
with its dismal history of enslavement and domination.

Consciously, I endeavor to be kind and a help, rather than a hindrance, in
all I do and say. I love to know every kind act and good deed reverberates
around the world and beyond! Deeply thankful indeed.

## – DAY 167 –

How glad I am to nurture honesty, sincerity and integrity within
as I keep consciously evolving.

A long time ago I could easily fool myself, and actually lie to me!
At that time, it was easy to believe the lies I told myself.

Not so anymore, thankfully.

Nowadays, I eke out any falsehoods or insincerity I might be hiding,
and it feels so much better.

I absolutely trust myself, to practice radical honesty with myself and
others, which leads to a sense of integrity and balance and peace
that I treasure.

## – DAY 168 –

Today I am grateful for second chances (and third);
When I receive them, and when I have the grace to offer them.

My life is enhanced by learning and relearning lessons;
to err is human, right?

How often do I have the grace to offer myself "do-overs"
and forgive myself when I act out in patterned behaviors, due to stress
or failed coping strategies?

I am worthy of unconditional
love and support;
Especially from myself!

## – DAY 169 –

*"To shine your brightest light is to be who you truly are."*
Roy T. Bennett

Today, as we move closer to the summer solstice, I celebrate and revel in the light – the light of the sun which plays, creating amazing reflections and shadows, the early morning light, the magical dusk, and oh-so-glorious sunsets.

And I know that the light within, the illumination that we all have when we don't let it be dimmed is the most dazzling radiant light of all.

I am so grateful to shine my own light brightly.

## – DAY 170 –

*"Each of us follows our heart until we realize
within ourselves that we need to change.
I will continue to look within at the metamorphosis
of the ever approaching dawn of my own light."*
Rick Terwilliger

Today, I give great thanks for the dawn of light in my heart.
It is here right now, and it is growing brighter day by day.
How grateful I am to realize that my light cannot be dimmed
unless I let it be.

I am awake, I am aware and I evolve each day.
I let my love and light shine outward!

*"Joy and peace in my heart, Always I feel
Joy and peace in my mind, God within revealed
Joy and peace in my mind, I am healed."*
Lyrics by Melissa Phillippe

I appreciate all the wise sages in my life
including beautiful New Thought singers.
They help me remember that I am not alone;
that I am part of the Divine;
and that all is truly well.

As I release my expectations and timetables for what I envision,
I am so grateful to feel that peace and joy and love
deep within my heart and soul.

*"In times of turmoil and danger, gratitude helps to steady and ground us.
It brings us into presence, and our full presence is perhaps the best offering
we can make to our world."*
Joanna Macy

Any time – morning, noon and night – I know that gratitude
enriches my life.
A steady diet of thankfulness helps fortify health, wealth,
love, peace and joy.
And when the going gets tough, I have seen from personal experience
that there is not a better time for counting blessings.
It can wake me up from sadness and fear!
As we amplify what is good and right, light beckons even in dark times.
So thankful to hold this golden key.

*"The further I wake into this life, the more I realize that God is everywhere
and the extraordinary is waiting quietly
beneath the skin of all that is ordinary."*
Mark Nepo

How beautiful it is to realize the Divine is in everything.
I am incredibly thankful to feel this deeply.
We couldn't be separate no matter how we try.

Every moment of every day is a blessed miracle of life.

I am forevermore grateful.

## – DAY 174 –

*"Love liberates. It doesn't just hold – that's ego – love liberates!"*
Maya Angelou

How thankful I am to love freely and joyously,
those whom I know intimately, those whom I know a little bit
and even those whom I've never met.

My mission is to love all and accept all, and the path to getting there is
truly loving myself.

I am grateful to set others free with my loyal, strong love!
I am grateful to see myself free as I cherish, honor and respect me.

Thank you for this day. Thank you for the air I breathe. Thank you for the gift of life. Thank you. Thank you for sunshine. Thank you for refreshing rivers. Thank you for the ancient redwoods.
Thank you for my own self-love. Thank you for birds flying high.
Thank you for this day. Thank you for the air I breathe. Thank you for the gift of life. Thank you. Thank you for the sweet oasis where we live.
Thank you for summer flowers a'bloom.
Thank you for the love and peace in my heart.
Thank you for this day. Thank you for the air I breathe. Thank you for the gift of life. Thank you.

Thank you, thank you, thank you!

Inspired by Jess Hesslop's wonderful gratitude meditation, www.ilivethelifeilove.com. (Thank you!)

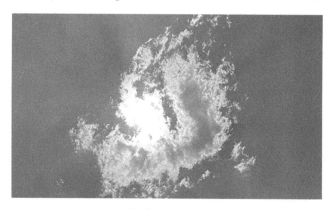

## – DAY 176 –

As clouds move in the sky, they are forever shape shifting.

I recall lying on the grass looking up at the clouds when a girl, marveling at how they didn't ever stay the same.

Seeing an animal or fairy or angel form in a cloud, or trying to blow them into a different shape with my mind, and sometimes it seemed to work.

I realize that I am sometimes too rigid, too stuck in my ways, and with all the changes in life, I can shift and be more adaptable, I can be more free-flowing, I can take a lesson from the clouds and allow life to unfold without a stubborn need to cling. I am thankful for letting go!

How grateful I am that I am definitely NOT in charge of the universe!
Sometimes I bear the burden of too much responsibility – I let my
personal self, not my higher self, chatter and complain and bemoan
situations. I can get very caught up with that inner voice, and forget the
bigger picture.

That part of me wants what she wants NOW even though I know there
is Divine timing. When I'm listening to my self-talk, I can feel weighted
down, like it is all up to me, which is ridiculous but feels real at times.

So, I surrender my petty wishes, and let go and remember Spirit is in charge.
Simultaneously, I do what I can to improve my life, and savor the core truth
that I am blessed with an abundance of good in every way.
So thankful.

– DAY 178 –

*"Roll out those lazy, hazy, crazy days of summer."*
Sung by Nat King Cole

The bliss of summertime is such a gift. I manage to take walks and swim at
the nearby river almost every day, and enjoy the surprise of new blooms in
our garden; the dappled sunlight through the forest; my beautiful girl dog
playing stick over and over (and over); and our other boy dog racing here
and there in unbounded joy.

The warmth and sunshine this July is perfect – it is not too hot,
but just right . . .

I truly appreciate all the seasons, but oh my God,
hallelujah to the summer!

*"So I say to you, walk with the wind, brothers and sisters, and let the spirit of peace and the power of everlasting love be your guide."*
John Lewis, in a letter written to all of us days before he died, July 2020

The Spirit of peace and love blows strongly within me and all of us when we let our true nature shine. Let us walk in love and light and transform the world with these powers.

In this time of a major reset, let us not go back to injustice and intolerance and judgment and division.

I am grateful to feel the power of kindness, of balance, of Oneness, of unconditional love that I know is the truth of our being.
Let's live it.

## – DAY 180 –

*"I wish I could show you, when you are lonely or in darkness, the astonishing light of your own being!"*
Hafiz

How grand it is to feel the Divine radiance of the All-That-Is, throughout all of life, and yes, within me.
When my light feels dim, I purposefully turn to what there is to be grateful for and then it grows brighter and brighter again, sparkling and shining.

And when I feel my inner light glow, I let it blaze outward to warm and comfort others' hearts.

I am so grateful for inner illumination.

*"The most enduring reward for kindness is our experience of Oneness.*
*For being kind renews our kinship with all things."*
Mark Nepo

Being kind is so important always, but especially at this juncture in our
human existence.
It is essential to be kind to ourselves, and then to extend it to all.

I am thankful to be naturally kind and caring and compassionate
and my biggest lesson is to be that to me.

Let us all be kinder, purposefully, each and every day
and let's remember the critters and every part of Mother Earth too!

## – DAY 182 –

The world is replete with mystery and magic if we take time to notice.
I am glad that I seek the beauty, I seek the love, I seek the harmony and
joy and peace.

And what I seek, lo and behold, I find!

I am thankful each day to discover something new to be grateful for.

I focus on the good and know there is more and more and more to find,
and lots of it is there right within my own open heart.

## – DAY 183 –

*"There is a very simple method for staying open. You stay open by never closing. It's really that simple. Closing is a habit, and just like any other habit, it can be broken."*
Michael A. Singer

I treasure and cherish my tender, open, loving heart.
And I am learning to let it stay open, no matter what.
Can you imagine if the whole world's people had open hearts?!

What a kind, loving, sharing, compassionate society it would be.
I am so thankful to be part of an evolving consciousness
that is changing the world!

## – DAY 184 –

How amazing every single day's dawn is!
I delight in the morning light each day. It is a reminder of the fresh new
possibilities we have each day;
it is a reminder of the beauty of every single moment.
It is a reminder that we live in a friendly universe
(despite any appearances to the contrary).

I celebrate dawn's golden light
and celebrate my beautiful sacred life!

And yes, I am thankful.

May my mind be clear like a river,
flowing like a river,
adaptable like a river.

Let me keep learning from the river's example – meandering
where life takes me, eroding barriers that stand in the way
and going with the flow, despite obstacles.

I am grateful for the lovely, effervescent waters of this world.
And so grateful they inform me.

– DAY 186 –

*"The truth is, everything will be okay as soon as you are okay*
*with everything."*
Michael A. Singer

I am utterly and ever thankful for my acceptance of things
beyond my own control.

And I realize there is nothing is in my control except for me!
Well-being and peace reside within me, always accessible when I enter
the silence and listen.

I celebrate knowing that all is okay, because I am okay.

So grateful.

*"We are part of a Mystery we do not understand, and we are grateful."*
Brian Doyle

Divinity is far, far more than I can fathom.
And it honestly thrills me that there is so much I cannot know.
Wouldn't it be boring if we understood everything about life,
including the afterlife?

I am thankful for each new understanding I gain in my spiritual studies,
and I am thankful for all that I do not know.

Life is a gift, and often a delightful surprise.
I cherish it.

## – DAY 188 –

*"Faith is the bird that feels the light and sings when the dawn is still dark."*
Rabindranath Tagore

I vow to have faith like a bird singing for the dawn before it's light.
I consciously shore up my faith and trust.

I tap into the Divine strength and guidance every single day, religiously.

I ward off thoughts of doubt and fear, which can be amplified when
looking at the state of the world and some people's actions,
yet I know without an iota of doubt that Oneness is the truth of life
and in that Oneness, we can know it all and I am deeply thankful.

*"You did not arrive on planet earth to be a consumer. You came here to be a generator of ideas by tapping into the Divine mind and affirming that you are one with the power and the presence and the love of God."*
Michael B. Beckwith

My idea of success has shifted . . . I used to believe it was having a lot of money and fame. Now I am grateful to know that what truly counts is being a creator of good, a beneficial presence on this planet. I know that loving people/plants/creatures/myself is what matters in the big picture.

I am thankful to continue creating ideas and thoughts that help,
not hinder, our human race,
always filled with the power of gratitude.

– DAY 190 –

I am ever grateful for listening to my heart, and usually much more than
my monkey-mind thoughts.

My intuition doesn't steer me wrong
even when it seems like I'm way off according to the rest of the world!

I stand strong in my inner knowing.

I stand strong in my connection to Spirit.

I stand strong in honoring myself, and what I glean from listening.

So very thankful.

## – DAY 191 –

The mellowing of my personality,
as I live more years on this Earth,
is a true gift and blessing.

The rough edges are smoothed,
like the colored glass you can find on a beach
that has been tossed and tumbled in
the ocean.

Thankful for all life's tumbling that has led me to today.

## – DAY 192 –

*"One of the most extraordinary aspects of our humanity is our capacity to
learn, grow, and change."*
Sheryl Chard

What a gift it is to change and adapt throughout my life.
I have evolved mightily!
Once a shy young girl who was reticent to talk, I speak my mind and
probably am not seen as shy. As a young woman, I felt "too cool" to
embrace all the different ways and ages of people,
leaving out opportunities to know wise elders,
and also wiser young people!
Since 2000, I have become a teacher and a gratitude aficionado
and I purposely choose to be a beneficial, bright, loving light in this world.
I am grateful I am never stuck and can always keep growing.

*"Faith is taking the first step even when you don't see the whole staircase."*
Martin Luther King Jr.

I am so grateful to grow my faith each and every day, consciously
and with intention.
As I do so, I let go of worry, which is the opposite of faith, letting it
dissolve, as I keep walking in faith, in trust, in certainty.

Like light, good overpowers darkness
and I am positive we live in a friendly universe
supported, guided, loved always.

Thank you.

– DAY 194 –

*"Just hug yourself and transcend any thought-forms about your
unworthiness, about not being good enough, about being unsupported by
the Universal presence; any thought-form that would in any way not be
in alignment with the absolute truth that you are cradled, enveloped, and
loved by a Presence that is never an absence."*
Michael B. Beckwith

One of my life's lessons is to know my worth, to be filled with self-love,
even when I make a mistake or do something that isn't "perfect."

I am responsible for me, and for tuning into my wise higher self where I
can access the expansive love that I truly am.

I am more than worthy! And I am deeply loved. Incredibly thankful.

## – DAY 195 –

*"For my yoke is easy, and my burden is light."*
Matthew 11:30

I am thankful for joy, for lightheartedness, for fun!
I am thankful when I don't take things so darn seriously;
when I take my nose off the grindstone, and relax into trust and faith
that all is truly well.

We are supported, guided and loved by the Great Creator/God/
The Universe always, and when I truly realize this, it feels so good
to lay my burdens down.

## – DAY 196 –

*"Reflection is the lamp of the heart.*
*If it departs, the heart will have no light."*
Imam Al-Haddad

I am indubitably grateful for the light shining from my heart,
and for the reflection and contemplation I choose to practice each day.

My soul reflects all the wisdom and love that comes from Spirit
and when I am feeling healed and whole,
I cast light in all directions.
When I go into fear or doubt or worry, the lamp dims.
I am thankful when my inner light shines brightly.

*"The life of spirit is everywhere: in dust waiting for light,*
*in music waiting to be heard, in the sensations of the day waiting to be felt.*
*Being spiritual is much more useful and immediate than the books about*
*books would have you think."*
Mark Nepo

It is so true and easy to forget that Spirit is alive and in everything, and in
everyone. When I pay attention and take time to breathe and be present,
I see this life reaching out to me, calling to me from every tiny plant,
in the new blossoms of spring fruit trees, and in the vast and infinite sky.

I have read many, many spiritual books
and the thing is, it is the practice, it is the noticing, it is the love and peace
and joy that I get from living life that truly matters. How grateful am I.

– DAY 198 –

*"The wisdom and beauty of Infinite Love & Gratitude*
*is all around you and within you, in the essence of your soul's longing*
*to experience life."*
Darren Weissman

Everywhere I look is a part of me, and I am a part of everything too.
If I ever feel alone or lonely, I can take comfort in this fact, and shift to joy
and peace.

I am thankful, so thankful, for connection, for unity,
for the vast and infinite Oneness that we are each an essential, precious,
unique part of. For me, it doesn't get much better than realizing how true
this is, and reminding myself through the power of constant appreciation.

## – DAY 199 –

*"All too many students are over-read and under-done."*
Eric Butterworth

I have read and read and read spiritual books galore –
many times rereading, and always getting something new
because I have transformed since the first time I read the wise words.
New passages get highlighted.

Yet, it is essential to LIVE the spiritual principles I read about. That is my
mission these days. To love freely, feeling compassion, being kind, letting
go of grievances and surrendering to what is. Key points for me.

I am grateful to realize that I am nicely done! More to learn, more to grow
into, but doing just fine.

## – DAY 200 –

*"One of life's most fulfilling moments occurs in the split-second when the
familiar is suddenly transformed into the dazzling aura of the profoundly new."*
Edward B. Lindaman

It thrills me when I find myself in the dazzling aura of new territory!
I forget time for a moment. I am immersed in the spirit world, and lose my
usual grounded self for that time.

Just a couple of examples. It happens when I swim in the river because
that is a place of joy and bliss for me. It occurs when I am teaching
spiritual workshops or classes because that is a calling for me.
When time stands still, all is made new!
I "wake up" and life is transformed into magic and awe and splendor.
I am grateful for those precious times that remind me how much more is
revealed that our eyes just cannot see.

One of my life's lessons is to know my worth, to be filled with self-love, even when I make a mistake or do something that isn't "perfect." I sometimes feel all alone, like everything is up to me. When really, truly, nothing is up to me, the world outside of myself is decidedly not in my control.

I am responsible for me, and for tuning into my wise higher self where I can access the expansive love that I am.

When mistakes are made, I forgive myself fully. I love myself deeply. Knowing I am more than worthy no matter what.

When I feel this and let it sink in, I am incredibly thankful.

## – DAY 202 –

*"We think that accomplishing things will complete us, when it is experiencing life that will."*
Mark Nepo

Someone who was working toward a goal confided in me that she didn't even notice the seasons because she was so focused on what she wanted to accomplish. Autumn leaves turned gold and orange and red, and fluttered to the ground around her, and she was completely oblivious.

I must admit I get really focused on my work at times, and miss the present moment. Yet now is the most important moment we have. I realize that in the big picture, it is essential to stop so much doing and just be. I give myself permission to notice the astounding nature around me, and to love and give and care more freely. I am so thankful to slow down and allow myself the chance to truly see.

## – DAY 203 –

*"May you grow still enough to hear the splintering of starlight
in the winter sky and the roar at earth's fiery core."*
Br. David Steindl-Rast

How exquisite is nature in every way, every day!
I am so thankful for the stillness of the night sky – for full moons and
clouds encircling them like last night.
I am grateful for the lacy, silhouetted winter bare trees that are resplendent
in their own quiet beauty.

When I get still, I notice so much more.
And I am grateful beyond measure for listening and observing the magic
and wonder and miracles that occur in every moment. Shhhhhh!

## – DAY 204 –

*"How grateful I am for my existence, for that of my loved ones, my
community, my country, and my world. Beauty and bountifulness are
everywhere present, reminders that I live in a world of opulence that
advertises Spirit's omnipresence."*
Michael B. Beckwith

Every day I give great thanks for the bountiful blessings in my life.
I love so much about this life, and bow down in gratitude for all the
blessings as well as the challenges. The challenges truly help me grow
emotionally and spiritually, even if I don't appreciate them at the time!

I am constantly in touch with the beauty and bounty of nature, which is
such a palpable reminder of all that Spirit provides,
as are all of the beautiful souls I am privileged to know. LIFE IS GOOD!

*"The best way to cheer yourself up is to try to cheer somebody else up."*
Mark Twain

How thankful I am for this practical solution!

It always works – it is the same with giving when I am down or temporarily feeling lack. Give and give generously; be kind, and there is often a boomerang effect. Lead with your heart, instead of your mind.

And lastly, unearth the gratitude!

This stuff works, folks, and I am so grateful to be the messenger.

## – DAY 206 –

*"I believe that unarmed truth and unconditional love will have the final word in reality. This is why right, temporarily defeated, is stronger than evil triumphant."*
Martin Luther King Jr.

Love is the elixir and balm that heals all.
I am in deep gratitude to know this.
There is always hope, always redemption, always the chance to start anew . . . creating a healing, peaceful me as I contribute to a healing, peaceful world.

I am so thankful for leaders, those alive, and those still alive with their powerful, oh-so-inspiring words and beliefs that reverberate on and on . . . The strongest leaders believe in the good of humans and hope for humankind. I resonate with their optimism.

*"It's our insides that make us who we are, that allow us to dream and wonder and feel for others. That's what's essential. That's what will always make the biggest difference in our world."*
Fred Rogers

If we live from the inside out, if we open our hearts and love more, we can affect the world in a beneficial way. We can be lights showing the way.

I stopped striving for "success" as defined by outside influences long ago. My definition of success is feeling joy, feeling peace, feeling loved and loving, feeling fulfillment through my creativity and all that I think, do and say. With this perspective, all my dreams and my sense of wonder expand in magnanimous ways.

– DAY 208 –

*"The journey of your spirit is to connect with the power of infinite love and gratitude."*
Darren Weissman

I am grateful to realize that what we can't see with our human eyes is much more real than what we can see.

I am thankful for the infinity of Divinity – the profusion of Presence that my spiritual eyes behold.

*"Our fears and terrors can be activated by the news, but they are not who we are. We are consciousness itself, loving awareness, born into this body and having a wild human ride. What will you do with this human dance?"*
Jack Kornfield

I truly love the wild ride of life!

I dance to the rhythm of my own heart and soul,
and my intention is to love fully, both myself and all others,
and to bring more joy and light into our world with my giving.

I dance to compassion, to kindness, to serving, to the good which is
always visible with the right perspective.
And I am deeply thankful.

– DAY 210 –

*"Trust yourself; you know more than you think you do."*
Benjamin Spock

It is my belief that since we are part of the All-in-All,
we have way more wisdom and knowledge to tap into than we realize.

We are part of the Divine – so there is omniscience to guide us.

There are the Akashic Records, which we can access if we open our
intuition and listen.

I am eternally thankful to feel faith and trust in me, and be sure that I have
answers within when I need them,
and I can count on that.

How thankful I am to be a person supercharged with energy,
with enthusiasm, with great vitality.

Of course it is not all the time, I am subject to conflicting emotions that
can bring me down from that high vibration.

But mostly, I live in the realms of high positive energy.
Lots of times, I am ready to take on the world!
And I credit my meditation and prayer time and all the wisdom I read
each day that fills me up with inner strength and power
and guess what, gratitude!
Hallelujah!

## – DAY 212 –

*"Perfectionism is the spinster who tells you, in mincing words,
that she has 'standards.'"*
Tama Kieves

This nagging spinster definitely resides within me, and if I let her,
she can put a halt to any new idea or endeavor I think up, because she expects
perfection and that is not a fair or realistic standard to set for a mortal.

My work is creative and I often have that nagging voice within me telling
me before I even finish a project that it's not good enough, and I'm not
good enough. I've been consciously letting go of my inner critic,
and feeling the subsequent excitement and thrill of allowing something
brand new to appear. As part of the Divine, I know that deep within, I am
perfect, whole and complete despite human flaws. Extremely grateful to
realize this and let it permeate my consciousness. Spinster, begone!

## – DAY 213 –

*"All things share the same breath – the beast, the tree, the man.*
*The air shares its spirit with all the life it supports."*
Chief Seattle, circa 1850

Indigenous peoples' age-old philosophy is so right-on. Their worldview
cherishes all, and sees all as interconnected, understanding that because
we are all a part of each other and everything around us, that doing no
harm makes complete sense. When making decisions, they consider what
is beneficial for the future seven generations.
I so believe with all my heart that if we lived by their tenets, giving to,
as well as taking from Mother Nature; feeling and speaking gratitude
morning, noon and night for all that Spirit gives us; we could heal the
Earth and live in harmony. I am grateful for all of the ancient wisdom
already imparted, and I strive to live it.

## – DAY 214 –

*"Whatever may be the tensions and the stresses of a particular day,*
*there is always lurking close at hand the trailing beauty of forgotten joy or*
*unremembered peace."*
Howard Thurman

I remember even when in the midst of stress, that this too shall pass.
And every morning dawns with a fresh, new beginning.

I am thankful to let go of past grievances or sorrows
and embrace the now moment – I know the present is a precious gift.

Here's to joy and peace and serenity!
My cup is full of all good when I let in the light and love
that is always here.

*"Praise and blame, gain and loss, pleasure and sorrow come and go like the wind. To be happy, rest like a giant tree in the midst of them all."*
Jack Kornfield

Stand strong like a tall tree with deep roots
amidst all the hubbub of the world.

I practice this ever-increasingly
as I realize emotions and outside happenings need not sway me.

I am rooted in the Divine, and I am strong and grounded
and ever-thankful.

**– DAY 216 –**

*"We are in moments pure and ageless as light, and with the very next breath, we drop things or bruise the treasures of a lifetime.
We need to soothe ourselves, not blame ourselves."*
Mark Nepo

I vow to treat myself gently with acceptance when I go off track into anger or upset after feeling spiritual bliss. My partner of 20 years especially knows how to push my buttons, and I let myself react. Yet, we are humans. If we didn't have things to learn, I believe we would transcend this life.

Every day, I am so blessed to feel moments of that agelessness, that purity, that blazing light and love, and then it can vanish so quickly when my egoic mind rears up. I am glad to know that perfection is sought after but not often actually attained, and that I am just right as I am.

## – DAY 217 –

*"The Divine Plan is one of Freedom.*
*The inherent nature of man is ever seeking to express itself in terms of*
*freedom, because freedom is the birthright of every living soul."*
Ernest Holmes

Freedom comes with our free will as humans. We are always at choice.
Yes, there is tyranny and power and struggle, I realize that,
but then I recall Anne Frank and Victor Frankl, and how they managed to
stay in gratitude even during the Holocaust.
We can stay free in our own heart and soul no matter what.

I am incredibly grateful for my personal freedom. I am thankful for
the freedom to love, to live, to be in joy, to be at peace, and to always
remember to be grateful.

## – DAY 218 –

*"The industry of distraction makes us forget*
*that we live in a universe."*
John O'Donohue

I am thankful to step out of the world's
interference, usually through the doorway
of nature, to remember the vast infinity and
unlimited possibilities that I am a tiny but
integral part of, as is every single one of us.

I couldn't be more grateful for the Universe and its vastness,
reminding me of what is important, not my mundane problems.

What a gift it is to feel deep trust, and have this quality within me grow exponentially as I consciously commit to a practice of trusting in Spirit. And I am shown, time and time again, that my trust is reciprocated in an overall sense of goodness, of well-being, of light, of peace, of joy. How sweet it truly is.

I trust the universe, I trust that everything I need is always supplied, and that there is a greater knowing that overrides any sense of worry or concern. The highest and best good IS occurring, even when I doubt that.

Deeply grateful for a gentle breeze of trust and faith always touching my heart and soul.

– DAY 220 –

*"At the height of laughter, the universe is flung into a kaleidoscope of new possibilities."*
Jean Houston

I definitely let myself get too serious sometimes.
Laughter is such healing medicine.
There is no reason to take every little thing so darn seriously, right?
And that's not to spiritually bypass grief or social injustice or maladies.
All this is worthy of tears and sorrow.

Yet, with a light and joyful heart, I laugh at all the absurdities of life.
I laugh at myself for obsessing over things I cannot change.
I laugh at my silly husband and our precious pooches, and with kindred souls too. Deeply thankful, I laugh at the joy to be found in each sacred moment.

*"What nature delivers to us is never stale.*
*Because what nature creates has eternity in it."*
Isaac Bashevis Singer

Everything, everyone, everywhere is part of nature.
And so we are each a slice of eternity.

No matter how temporary things may seem in the temporal world,
we can always count on the eternal.

I am so grateful to be reminded of this, and to let it be ingrained
into my awareness.

– DAY 222 –

I am so thankful to know that a way to turn a gray, down mood in a
sunnier, more joyful direction is to give.

It feels so good to give, whether it is praise, support, time, creativity
or appreciation or even money . . .

I can and do find ways to give when feeling depleted, and it fills me up
to do so.

Thankful for giving as well as receiving!

Thankful for Divine circulation!

*"Looking through the lens of appreciation, I see the world in a new light;*
*clear and crisp rather than cloudy and obscure.*
*Just as I can change the focus on a camera with a simple turn,*
*I can change the focus of my life with the simple practice of gratitude."*
Unity Daily Word, February 11, 2020

How grand it is to shift my world with my attitude of gratitude.
Time and time again, I pivot away from what doesn't feel good
to what I am thankful for. And it works! My vibration returns to the beauty,
magic, wonder of life itself!

I am beyond grateful for this powerful, spiritual tool.

– DAY 224 –

How grateful I am to be truly free!
I celebrate freedom in so many ways in my life:
freedom to express myself; the freedom to live life how I want to live it;
freedom to enjoy inner peace no matter what;
freedom to be joyful, to be lighthearted, to be silly;
freedom to love and care and lavish my love toward others and to me;
freedom to stay strong in my spiritual beliefs, that help me to navigate
unknown territories; freedom to stretch my boundaries and to explore . . .

Most of all, I appreciate my free will that is God-given.
I am free to make choices in every minute of my life.

And when it appears I am not as free as I would like,
I affirm my absolute independence and I am thankful.

*"I am filled with unlimited strength."*
Unity Daily Word, October 6, 2020

As I connect with Divinity within me, I feel strong, I feel free, I feel ready
for whatever life may toss my way.
I am utterly thankful that I am never alone, it is not always up
to little ol' me.

I am guarded, guided, supported and protected by a higher loving power.

How grand it is to be mighty when I access the power within.
Yes!

**– DAY 226 –**

*"Gratitude doesn't change everything, but it does change YOU.
And when you change, everything becomes different."*
Jennifer Williamson

I am thankful that my grateful heart amplifies and welcomes in the good in
life. And I am grateful for change – I feel there is a sea change coming,
and we humans can and will shift and metamorphize into a more loving
consciousness. I am grateful to do my part.

Where there is hate in my own heart, I seek to transmute it.
Where there is conflict within me, I choose peace.
Change is a'coming – it is a constant we can count on in
our human existence and today, right now, I welcome more and more
extravagant good.

I am ever-grateful to be grounded in God, the All-That-Is, the Oneness. From this vantage point, I am filled with light, with love, with peace and sweet serenity.
It sounds simple but staying there is the rub.

Living in the forest helps me stay grounded, and going within is precious. Being with an earthy person like my husband or a good friend's help can keep me tethered too.

Turning off the news is paramount.

When I stay grounded, I am in balance and all is well.
So thankful.

## – DAY 228 –

Great gratitude for all the mystery of life. The unseen, the magic, the lavish abundance and creativity of Spirit! When children, most of us were told magic didn't really exist, and some of us forgot our dreams, but magic exists – in the birth of life on this planet – not only our world's beginnings so long ago but in humans and mammals and crustaceans and plants and on and on and on; in the knowing of the seasons to change at exactly the right time; in the gazillions of stars so ancient in the sky; in the power and supreme beauty of all of nature.

Magic exists in the unseen of life; in love, in silent but telepathic communication; and in the mystery of other dimensions not visible to most of us yet.

We truly live in a magical multiverse!

*"Things are not always what they seem; the first appearance deceives many; the intelligence of a few perceives what has been carefully hidden."*
Phaedrus

Oh, it is so amazing how things are not always what they appear on the surface. Each of us a masterpiece of creation, and each of us have struggles that don't always show.

I am incredibly grateful for grace and beauty.
I am thankful for mystery and magic and awe.
Life is stellar and astounding.

– DAY 230 –

*"With an eye made quiet by the power of harmony, and the deep power of joy, we see into the life of things."*
William Wordsworth

When distracted by the chatter within my mind, I can miss the beauty and wonder of all that surrounds me. When I take walks, I can be in another world within my own mind, not noticing anything around me.

When I get still and am present, I am filled with serenity and joy, and I notice even the smallest miracles that are ever-present. Thankful for the Divine Presence within that helps me see aright.

## – DAY 231 –

*"If things aren't going your way, personality panics
while character remains unruffled and learns from the experience."*
Michael B. Beckwith

How grateful I am for my spiritual journey.
My personality easily panics, and then my essence soothes me.
I can actually be in gratitude for lessons and challenges presented to me
knowing that as I grow in wisdom, my growth is accelerating by all that
occurs in my life. And I am thankful for almost always realizing that I am at
choice in how I respond to all situations and occurrences.

There is a wonderful saying "Respond with Love" and my aim is to
remember this and live it.

## – DAY 232 –

*"The best and most beautiful things in the world cannot be seen or even
touched – they must be felt with the heart. I thank God for my handicaps.
So much has been given me, I have no time to ponder over
that which has been denied."*
Helen Keller

It is so inspiring to me to realize how so much that I love about life
is found in the unseen.
Love, joy, peace, inner beauty, angels, those who have passed from
this Earth yet live on, Spirit or God or Higher Power, grace, kindness,
inspiration and creativity.
Some of these beautiful qualities manifest into the seen,
but they start out invisible.
I celebrate in gratitude all that can't be seen or heard or tasted!

*"Look closely at the present you are constructing; it should look like the future you are dreaming."*
Alice Walker

How completely grateful I am to watch what I am dreaming
come to fruition.

There is such power in knowing we can manifest what we desire,
if we don't hang it up with conflicting thoughts, or a belief
that we don't deserve.

I firmly believe in the potential of visualizing and visioning, and I delight in
watching as Life says yes.

– DAY 234 –

*"Sometimes, I move between resistance and surrender all day long.*
*If I can bring any amount of gratitude to what is right in front of me,*
*then some opening and release is possible.*
*It's as though waking up to surrender, allows my life to be infused*
*with more grace and gratitude."*
Colette Lafia

I am grateful for the path of least resistance – a path I am consciously
traveling more each day.
Letting go when I am butting into feelings of resistance is so freeing.
I am incredibly thankful to practice sweet surrender.

Acceptance is a gift I give myself.

*"Your inner glow comes from the light of God, and your light can never be extinguished. You are eternally bright and beautiful!"*
Doreen Virtue

How glad I am to feel that glow at times, and then to shine it outward.
I am grateful for the bright light from Spirit within
that illuminates my path.

I am reminded, and so glad, that light will always extinguish darkness
and not vice versa.

The light and love of God surrounds and permeates me and you.
Feel it and know it and shine ever brighter.

## – DAY 236 –

*"I am made of all the same stuff that makes the seasons what they are."*
Heather Maloney

Just like seasons, our lives change and transform.
The spring of our lives starts at birth, and into our childhood – fresh, new
and exciting. Teenage years and our 20s perhaps summer – lively and
mostly sunny. Middle age feels like autumn, when we are harvesting the
bounty we have created. And our wise aging years are like winter, when
we have learned to be still and rest.

But spring lives on in my mind!
I am constantly born anew, like the seasons.
We are a composite of all we have gone through, plus so much more.
Wow! I am incredibly grateful for every season of my life
and for my eternal life too.

## – DAY 237 –

*"Death is the landlord and you are the tenant."*
Michael A. Singer

Let me remember this as days go by . . . I am renting this life on Earth!
It is fleeting and temporary, and we just never know when death will come
calling. Let me not take my beautiful life for granted, let me live in the
present moment and savor all that life presents, just the way it is, and just
the way it is not.

It is all perfect. Challenges are for learning, I see this on deeper levels than
ever before. The joyful, loving, easier times are grand and as I live in the
now, I appreciate them more.
I live in peace and bliss, and honor the Divine which brought me here.

## – DAY 238 –

*"Gratitude before me and behind me.*
*Gratitude to the left of me and to the right of me.*
*Gratitude above and below me. Gratitude within and all around me."*
Angeles Arrien

I am grateful for gratitude reaching to infinity!
The opportunity to be grateful is everywhere and in everything,
if we allow ourselves to recognize all that the miracle of life is.

I am grateful for every little, tiny lifeform, all people, and for the most
gigantic forms of life, such as nebulas and black holes and spiral galaxies,
and the universe upon universe that go on forever.

And I am grateful for me!

*"Don't plan it all. Let life surprise you a little."*
Julia Alvarez

I appreciate understanding that life will surprise me,
I just never really know what comes next,
despite all my planning and tending to micromanage.
I am grateful to accept things as they are, and just as they are not.
I am grateful to know I might as well practice acceptance
in matters outside myself.
We really don't have a choice even though we may try to fight it.

Thank you for life's unexpected precious jewels!

## – DAY 240 –

Thank you, Spirit, for the ever-changing
material world. Everything flows, moves
and changes, so that one seemingly stuck
situation smooths itself out, naturally.

Human life is like a flowing river, and the
Changeless, the Unseen, the Soul is a
deep lake.

I am so grateful I can depend on the still waters
of the Divine.

*"Those who are certain of the outcome can afford to wait, and wait without anxiety . . . Patience is natural to those who trust."*
A Course in Miracles

I am the type of person who traditionally hurries, pushes
and does my best to make things happen.

Patience has been a learned character trait and honestly,
I still struggle sometimes.

Michael Beckwith has a great saying that helps me:
"Waiting is not God's denial."
Thank you for my trust in Divine right timing.

– DAY 242 –

Thank you for this beautiful, spectacular,
fantastic brand new day.

I am grateful to be alive.

I am grateful for my inner joy,
my inner peace.

I am grateful for the love and light
of Life expressing everywhere!

I am grateful to go with the flow . . .
to let go of my tendency to want what I want when I want it,
and to let the ebbs and flows of life carry me along instead
of swimming in the opposite direction
thereby making things harder for myself.

There is a natural progression of each day, of each season, of each year . . .
a time to rest and a time of activity . . .
a balance between doing and being.

How thankful I am to listen to my inner guidance
and heed Divine right order and timing.

– DAY 244 –

With all my heart, I give thanks for my spiritual family,
which keeps on growing year by year.

I connect with my beloved, loving peeps
at the Sunday services we attend.

We study wisdom together, we share deeply,
and together we expand our hearts and minds.

Such a blessing to embrace the like-minded in my life.

*"When you feel yourself breaking down, may you break open instead.
May every experience in life be a door that opens your heart, expands your
understanding, and leads you to freedom."*
Elizabeth Lesser

It is said that when one door closes, another opens. And in my own life,
I have found that to be true.

Each door closing (divorce, move from one state to another, changing
jobs) led to a beautiful, enriching new opportunity. I am grateful for
keeping my heart open, and my spirit willing as I deal with big change,
and to be brave enough to go through open new doors.

– DAY 246 –

*"The sun, with all those planets revolving around it and dependent on it,
can still ripen a bunch of grapes as if it had nothing else
in the universe to do."*
Galileo Galilei

Thank you for the Divine right order of the universe!

For the miracles of life that abound everywhere and in everything.

Nature always knows exactly what to do
and does not worry or fuss.

*"Creating spaciousness in our minds and in our physical environments*
*makes room for stillness and peace.*
*A quiet mind is like a clean, blank page. Contemplate possibility. Allow*
*dreams to take place."*
Emily Silva

I bask in the serenity of the early dawn silence.
I am so grateful to start my days in spaciousness.
As I pray and meditate and make intentions for each new day,
I am conscious that I am welcoming my dreams to manifest
in stillness and in peace.

– DAY 248 –

*"Plant yourself so deeply in gratitude*
*that even the greatest of landslides cannot*
*shake your peace."*
Nicole Addison

I am grounded in gratitude, my roots sturdy and strong,
and usually unshakable.

How glad I am to be a person filled with thanksgiving
for all of life, the ups (of course), but even the downs,
as they teach me invaluable lessons when I pay attention.

*"Wisdom comes with the ability to be still. Just look and just listen. No more is needed.*
*Let stillness direct your words and actions."*
Eckhart Tolle

Easier said than done, right? In this often hectic world, I so appreciate the times of stillness I invite.
And I know in the quiet, if I listen, I do know just what to say and do.
That beautiful still small voice is deep within me.
I am grateful to listen deeply.
I let the mind chatter subside
and there is that grand overarching loving peace I so treasure.

– DAY 250 –

I am incredibly grateful for serenity,
that deep, abiding sense of peacefulness.
When I turn within, to my heart and soul,
I can find it. It is there.

And often, I also find bliss and joy.

How thankful I am that the Divine Creator
installed this into the operating system of each of us.

This is not to negate or ignore sad or grief-filled times.
But I know that deep within me lies serene omniscience,
even in the challenges.

*"My religion is nature. That's what arouses those feelings of wonder and mysticism and gratitude in me."*
Oliver Sacks

Nature is definitely the easiest opening for me to remember the grand
Divinity we are all immersed in . . .
and with that remembrance, I feel the magic, the wonder
and the mysticism
that is right there in front of us all the time.

How utterly grateful I am to notice the majesty of life
here, there and everywhere.

– DAY 252 –

I am incredibly grateful for absolute trust and faith
in the All Good of God,
demonstrating in every way, every single day in my life.

I know that as I believe, I receive.

Simple, true and yet, not always easy to stay grounded in this knowing.

When I give freely, I invite more and more good in abundant measure,
both to receive and to give again.

*"When you realize there is nothing lacking,
the whole world belongs to you."*
Lao Tzu

As I grow in gratitude, I know that my life is not lacking in any way.

A short list includes an abundance of joy, peace, love, well-being,
creativity; an abundance of friends and family;
and a plethora of comfort and food, and all that I could ever need.

My life is filled with plenty, and it starts within me.
I know there is always, always something to be grateful for
and I eke it out, even in challenges and struggles.

– DAY 254 –

*"I am a yes person living in a yes world, being responded to by a yes
universe, and I rejoice that this is so."*
Louise L. Hay

I must admit I am not always a yes person, especially when the world is
not cooperating with what I expect (COVID 2020 pandemic comes to
mind) and sometimes throws out curveballs.
Yet with acceptance and surrender tools in my spiritual toolbox, I am
grateful to be all in all an affirming, positive, optimistic person.

Even when my first inclination is to say no, I end up saying yes
to the all-good of this splendid life.

YES!

## – DAY 255 –

*"So just as we need to dust our homes, we need an inner practice
to dust our mind of all the webs we spin."*
Mark Nepo

Sometimes I find my mind is filled with cobwebs. They can be from past experiences and patterns I haven't let go of. For me, I have a cobweb of worry, and
another of telling myself I'm not good enough, that are hard to dust away.

With my spiritual practice, which includes reading wise sages' words,
study, meditating and prayer, I houseclean the inner workings of my inner
home every single day.

It feels so good to have a non-cluttered mind.
I am thankful as always for the tools to set myself free.

## – DAY 256 –

*"Paying attention is one of the kindest things we can do –
for ourselves, for others."*
Sharon Salzberg

I bask in gratitude for the Presence, and for my ability to be present
and still.

When I do, I listen, I am open, I am paying attention
and in this space, I am giving and offering the loving gift of attentiveness.

So thankful.

*"I AM a tower whose radiance is the inspiration to pen itself in its Divinity*
*in every shape and name through infinity.*
*I think this – I speak this – I write this – I live this."*
Emma Curtis Hopkins

Within every single one of us is radiant light and love. I AM that.
Within every single one of us lies creativity, imagination and omniscience.
I AM that.
We are perfect Divine beings having a human experience. I AM that.

How amazing it is, how grand it is to know I can, with inspiration, pen a
bright today and a luminous tomorrow.
Infinite gratitude reverberates from my heart and soul
for the magnificence of existence.

## – DAY 258 –

*"I was willing to roll the dice and let the flow of life be in charge."*
Michael A. Singer

It is amazing to watch what life has in store for me,
when I don't try to organize life as I am prone to want to do.
I am so grateful for SWEET SURRENDER,
for letting go, going with the flow and observing what comes next,
instead of resisting.

By getting out of the way, and trusting,
the Universe not only always has my back, but gifts me with blessings
beyond what I can imagine.

YES.

*"Gratitude is not in the words but in the heart which expresses it."*
Luffina Lourduraj

How thankful am I to let my heart guide me. I treasure what my heart
feels and knows even more than my logical, analytical mind.
This goes against society's dictates, I know.

So much that is powerful and true is invisible,
like love and peace and joy and harmony and wholeness,
to name some things we can't see or touch but are so integral
to a rich life. I am grateful for my open, intuitive heart. I am grateful for
trusting my inner wisdom to truly see.

– D A Y  2 6 0 –

*"Like a painting, every process has fine details we cannot see,*
*but they contribute to the bigger picture.*
*Perspective depends on where you stand in the process."*
Emily Silva

I am so thankful to be able to see the Big Picture, rather than get lost in
the brushstrokes of the painting of my life.
I am able to stand back and appreciate the fine vista; the overarching
perspective – the absolute beauty and splendor of a well-lived life.

I let go of worrying or fretting about day-to-day minutia,
knowing and feeling that I am cradled, cloaked and cherished
with Divine love and serenity.

*"Time and again I was seeing that if I could handle the winds of the current storm, they would end up blowing in some great gift."*
Michael A. Singer

I am filled with gratitude for every time I can watch what the Universe sends my way, with surrender, with assurance, with absolute confidence that it knows what it's doing much better than me.

And I delight in the gifts presented to me when I can let go of my preconceived notions of what "should" be.

I am so thankful for the bountiful gifts of Spirit.

– DAY 262 –

*"It is time for us to take what we've learned through the laws of attraction and begin using those creative powers to reunite humanity, heal the spiritual and psychic wounds we've created, and begin the process of healing Mother Earth."*
Sherri Mitchell

I am thankful for new-yet-ancient ideas and concepts that I embrace as I read sage wisdom. A recent amazing aha came to me when I read about the idea that instead of using the Law of Attraction for personal gain, we can use it to create the world as we want to be.

In ancient times, our awareness was tied to the Oneness of Life and our notions of success were aligned with the success of the whole.

This resonates on deep levels for me. In great gratitude, I shift my focus to the all, instead of just me-me-me.

*"All gain comes from a loss. All Spiritual growth and unfoldment
is letting go of something, and allowing That which is here,
That which is impervious to time and space, to show Itself."*
Michael B. Beckwith

It is truly beneficial to realize that growth and a revealing of something
new are natural effects of our feelings of loss.
We can let ourselves feel the Invisible Presence, and delve into
appreciation for the unseen forces
that are unaffected by the temporal concerns of the day.
How grateful I am for the omniscient, omnipresent, omniactive power of
the universe that is always creating and constantly expanding.
I am thankful to let go of status quo.

## – DAY 264 –

*"We must continually choose love in order to nourish our souls and drive
away fear, just as we eat to nourish our bodies and drive away hunger."*
Elisabeth Kübler-Ross and David Kessler

My aim is to always choose love, and I sometimes fall short!
It is true, I believe, that whatever is not love is actually fear, when we get
to the heart of it.
I aim to be a love ambassador, choosing love here and there and
everywhere, even when met with dislike or unacceptance or judgment.

I smile to think of love expanding and expanding, into more and more
hearts, so we can feel our intrinsic connection, not the separation.
We need each other, that's how humans are set up.
I am so thankful to cherish my loving heart.

*"He who kisses the joy as it flies lives in Eternity's sunrise."*
Steven Mitchell

I savor joy, I rejoice in joy, I find joy in the simplest things.

And when I'm not feeling it, I go to what I can rely on to lift my mood, and that is to recount what I am grateful for.

Joy is always within me, even when I have to coax it out.

And how grand to know that when I kiss it, I am dwelling in the beauty of eternity.

## – DAY 266 –

*"Take your stand as a spiritual revolutionary and participate in a revolution of values as you cultivate a heart of love as wide as the world."*
Michael B. Beckwith

I am thankful to know I don't have to blindly follow the crowd
and acquiesce to circumstances, thoughts and feelings
that go against who I am at the core.

I take a stand as a beneficial presence on this Earth.
I open my heart of love just as wide as I possibly can.

In deep gratitude for authenticity, and for being exactly who I am.

*"Just as life holds nothing back from me, I hold nothing back from life."*
Michael B. Beckwith

How glad I am to be a giver, as well as a receiver.

I realize that I am always abundantly, magnificently supplied by Spirit
with every single thing I can imagine.

And I give freely of my time, treasures, creativity, joy and love.

I am grateful to appreciate the law of circulation and to reside
in the Divine flow.

– DAY 268 –

*"May the nectar of kindness touch our lips as we speak,*
*may we find in ourselves the vast blue sky of inclusiveness*
*and may our hands turn the wheel of time toward a more just world, a*
*more beautiful world, a world worthy of our holy lives."*
Larry Ward

Wow, may my heart be filled with kindness expressed, and the knowing of
our absolute Oneness.

I am grateful to be a part of a concerted effort to create a better world,
more love-filled and holy, replete with justice and equality.
We can do it, one person at a time.
Let's.

It is heartening to see myself evolve and grow . . . when a situation is no longer working in my life, I am able to gracefully release it.

As an example, recently a person I've been working for was in the habit of blaming me, and not taking responsibility for her part, and it kept feeling bad. I knew what my part was in the situation, and realized this morning that I want to work with people who don't need to blame others.

I felt so light and free after letting her know I wouldn't be working for her anymore that I know my decision is right.

I am grateful to let go of needless suffering!

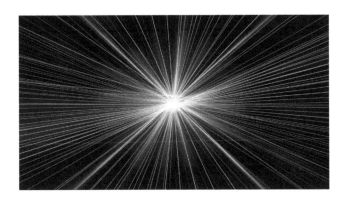

*"Whatever is in me is stronger than what is out there to defeat me."*
Caroline Myss

How thankful I am to know there is always a wellspring of inner strength for me to draw on.

I am strong, I am mighty, I am powerful!

No matter what happens in the outer world, my inner world is one of grace, serenity, peace and courage. I face whatever comes with resolve, energy and strength.

With Spirit always with me, I know I am invincible. So glad and grateful.

*"The sheer magnitude, and stubborn persistence, of this desire for*
*something different than what is can overwhelm us. It is clearly the captain*
*of our ship when we are asleep at the wheel."*
Gail Andersen Stark

How grateful I am to accept what is, exactly as it is.
And yes, it can be a challenge.
My ego wants to fight and rebel.
The Divine within me is filled with acceptance and tolerance and serenity.

I am thankful to choose peace when I am conscious that I have choices,
and I am thankful that I always do.

– DAY 272 –

*"Fluidity and discontinuity are central to the reality*
*in which we live."*
Mary Catherine Bateson

I am so grateful for fluidity –
for flowing easily with life's changes;
for being lighthearted and filled with grace.

I am thankful for my ability to let go and let God . . .
which is so much easier than resisting
and thinking I know what's best!

*"In the end, maybe it's wiser to surrender before the miraculous scope of human generosity and to just keep saying thank you, forever and sincerely, for as long as we have voices."*
Elizabeth Gilbert

I am constantly in awe of the fact that being grateful soothes my soul if I feel off or down . . . that there are an infinite number of reasons to be thankful, as infinite as the universe upon universe we abide in.

My cup is always overflowing when I bow down in gratitude for all that is, and even all that is not exactly how I want it to be.

Gratitude is an oh-so-positive habit, and it's hard to abolish once you engage in the practice.

– DAY 274 –

*"Living through the heart is where we are all going, sooner or later, someday, in some lifetime."*
Jonathan Goldman

I remember when I met Jonathan (and his assistant) to talk about the possibility of me designing *Gift of the Body*, his amazing book, after talking to me briefly, he told me "We go by our hearts and we choose you." I remember being glad they chose me, and also VERY inspired about what they said about using their hearts to decide on a business matter.

Since then, I let my intuition and inner guidance from my heart steer me as much as possible. As my journey in this lifetime goes on, more and more I know on deep levels I can trust my heart and intuition. I am very grateful to let my heart lead me, using doses of common sense, of course.

## – DAY 275 –

My spirit is light and free.

And I let go of any heavy thoughts and burdens, letting them fly away.

I tap into the lightness and freedom that I can always feel, deep within me,
and I let it shine as the predominant feeling in my heart.

I am joy.
I am peace.
I am love
and I am dazzling light.

So very thankful.

## – DAY 276 –

*"I am free to create my life just the way I want.
I am grateful for my freedom."*
Eugene D. Holden

Sometimes choices can be daunting.
Yet, we are always free to choose.
I am thankful for my free will,
and grateful to use it wisely,
in an abundance of love and peace well-being!

*"Spiritual growth means increasing your awareness of beauty,
opening your heart, and experiencing more love and compassion."*
Sanaya Roman

Recently, I had an opportunity to shift – from judgment, disapproval and feeling like I was right – to a more open heart; to feeling on deep levels more compassion and love.

It teaches me, again, that the energy to focus on comes from my heart.
It does not come from the inner judge.
It is obvious which feelings I prefer by the peace and well-being I feel when I let go of judgment and melt into acceptance.

So much good abounds, we just have to pay attention. Very thankful.

– DAY 278 –

*"Let it be, let it be
Let it be, let it be
Whisper words of wisdom
Let it be."*
The Beatles

As I get stronger on my spiritual path, I know that letting it be is paramount to peace of mind. I embrace good ol' surrender, which used to be more of a struggle in my younger years.
I am deeply grateful to change myself when appropriate, and to know and accept what I cannot change.
I am deeply grateful to listen to this oh-so-beautiful Beatles song and to heed the gentle advice.

*"Grief and gratitude are kindred souls, each pointing to the beauty of what
is transient and given to us by grace."*
Patricia Campbell Carlson

I am grateful to allow myself to feel the whole spectrum of my emotions.
They do pass, of that I can be certain.
So I grieve today, letting myself feel the deep sadness of loss.
And I feel thankful for the support, caring, love and compassion that is in
my life, both from beloved friends and family.
And I know I am also held in the loving arms of Spirit.

There is grace in grief, and grace in gratitude,
and I am very thankful.

– DAY 280 –

Thinking of my earlier life before I found out how potent gratitude is,
I was kind of a spoiled complainer!
And I had absolutely nothing to gripe about! (just like now)

How grand it is to celebrate all that is good and right, focusing on the
abundance of blessings that are always here.

How grand it is to be an optimistic dreamer, even in such a crazy world.

How simple, yet sometimes challenging it is,
to stay in the vibration of gratefulness.

I am ever-thankful to know of this powerful practice and to stay steady on
the path, no matter what.

*"Just admit when alone that the Atlas in your mind is tired
and wants to rest."*
Mark Nepo

I don't know if everyone has an Atlas in their mind but I certainly do,
sometimes believing the weight of the world is on my shoulders.
It is so not true! There is support and guidance available whenever I listen
to my inner wisdom.
There is support and guidance from those I know too.

I am so grateful to take life's burdens off my weary shoulders,
and rest in the knowledge that it's not all up to me.

– DAY 282 –

*"I do believe that the single most important thing I could ever, ever share
with you, with regard to maximizing the health, harmony, and happiness
in your life, not to mention expediting the manifestation of your heart's
fondest desires, can be summed up in just one word: Love yourself.
Okay, two words. Love yourself all of the time."*
The Universe a.k.a. Mike Dooley

I am grateful beyond measure to realize there is a Higher Power than me,
in this universe, that supports me, guides me, and loves me all of the time.
And knowing that helps me love me.
Filled with that love, I shine my love outward on all around me . . .
to those I am very close to, and those who are farther away.
I am thankful to say that I truly love myself almost all of the time!
and that is good enough for me.

*"Our inner wisdom is persistent, but quiet.*
*It will always whisper, but it will never stop knocking at your door."*
Vironika Tugaleva

I am thankful for persistent inner whispering.

It keeps me on track, it keeps me safe,
it keeps my path forward illuminated.

In the sacred silence, I listen.
And I hear what I need to hear, especially when I ask.

– DAY 284 –

*"Each of us has a dark side, along with our own grace and light. The extent*
*to which we can acknowledge the former while maximizing the latter*
*may determine how we choose to fulfill the terms of our Soul Contract."*
Caroline Myss

Although people I know applaud me for my light and love and peaceful
nature, I am painfully aware that I can erupt in anger with my husband,
and that I am hard on my own self too. The dark side shows up,
sometimes when I least expect it. But now I acknowledge it is there
instead of sugarcoating who I am, or trying to somehow extinguish the
shadow part of me.

How glad I am to be a whole, integrated person
experiencing good days, bad days and days in between.

*"Nothing in the world is as soft and yielding as water. Yet for dissolving the hard and inflexible, nothing can surpass it."*
from the Tao Te Ching

Rivers, lakes, streams and oceans are just about my favorite part of Mother Nature. When I float or swim in water, I feel so light and free.

And I witness water's power in riverbank erosion – how each year, the land around the river changes, often dramatically.
And there is incredible power in the ocean's waves tumbling and crashing.

In my own nature, I am grateful to be kind and gentle and giving, and filled with determination, energy and inner strength.
I am thankful to emulate the qualities of water.

– DAY 286 –

*"When life feels too big to handle, go outside. Everything looks smaller when you're standing under the sky."*
L.R. Knost

Perspective is so valuable. If I look at something bothering me as if through a microscope, it gets larger. If I go ahead and step back, and ponder a bigger picture, it shrinks in importance.

How grateful I am to let a larger perspective guide me, so I am not too caught up with everyday travails. I know that our existence is such a tiny blip in the eons of time the Earth and the universe have been here.

In great thanksgiving, I step outside and gaze at the grandeur of the cosmos, grateful that we are all connected and I am one with all that is.

## – DAY 287 –

I am ever so grateful for
INSPIRATION...
for me, one way it comes is through witnessing the supreme beauty of
creation. I am inspired, in awe, in constant wonder, of all the magical
goings-on abounding everywhere I look.

Inspiration also comes through meditation and contemplation . . .
where I am reminded what is truth for me, and feel the joy it inspires:
that we are all connected, that the power of love supersedes fear,
and that to hurt anything hurts me.

I am inspired by many lit-up luminaries in this world, who walk their talk, and
show me by who they are how to live a good life *of integrity.* How glad I am to
let the world and its occupants, including the blessed animals, inspire me.

## – DAY 288 –

I am grateful for all the times I treat myself tenderly – when I make a
mistake or act in a less-than-gracious way,
or eat food that doesn't serve me, or feel lazy and find excuses
for not exercising.

When I practice self-love, I can forgive myself like it is so easy to forgive
my friends and family.

I am, and we all are, tender beings
despite bravado or shields we put up to protect ourselves.

Today, I celebrate my tender, loving heart.

*"Each soul is a gust of God's breath unfolding
in the great energy that surrounds us
like an ever-moving stream."*
Mark Nepo

How fulfilling it is to understand that each person and each creature is
part of the soul of God–Goddess–All-That-Is. (And I wholeheartedly believe
that every tree and plant and flower has a soul as well.)
When allowing myself to deeply feel unity and harmony, rather than
separation and division,
I am grateful to recognize that all are gusts of Spirit's breath;
and there is power and majesty everywhere I turn.
Wow!

– DAY 290 –

*"This being human is a guest house. Every morning a new arrival.
A joy, a depression, a meanness, some momentary awareness comes as an
unexpected visitor. Welcome and entertain them all!"*
Rumi

I realize that all emotions are transitory, and everything in the material
world is changing all the time.
How very grateful I am to learn
ACCEPTANCE
and to welcome my guests no matter who they are.

I love and accept myself with all of my shifting moods –
good, bad or indifferent.

*"Consider all phenomena to be dreams. Be grateful to everyone.
Don't be swayed by outer circumstances. Don't brood over the fault of
others. Explore the nature of unborn awareness. At all times, simply rely on
a joyful mind. Don't expect a standing ovation."*
Atisha

Each day I find amazing inspiration from wise souls in my morning
contemplation time. I could not be more thankful. There is always a
pearl of beauty and wisdom awaiting me. Earlier in my life, I felt it was
imperative to get recognition or admiration or kudos from others. While
that is still a lovely gift when it happens, I am able to give my own self
recognition at a job well done, or an emotional thorn in my side pulled
out. And if I need a standing ovation, I can turn to my angels and guides
who are my own personal cheering squad. Yay, team!

*"If we could see clearly, we would recognize that every moment in life
contains an opportunity to see or understand something more clearly
than we did before."*
Caroline Myss

It's taken me over 50 years (better late than never), to see everything that
happens whether "good" or "bad" IS a means to understand life better.

What I adamantly know I don't want is a way for me to see what I do.

I watch all the transitory events and feelings and even people strut through
my life and they all show me parts of myself, and teach me more about
this phenomenal world. Life is a school and we are never done learning.
And I am mightily grateful this is so.

*"At first dreams seem impossible, then improbable, then inevitable."*
Christopher Reeve

I am happy to hold on to my dreams and visions.
If I don't let go, and keep envisioning, they manifest!

Spirit knows no small or big, so no matter how impossible they may seem
at first, we grow into them, I have found.

That is a gift I am very grateful for.

I am thankful to be a dreamer and watch the results transpire!

– DAY 294 –

*"It may be that some little root of the sacred tree still lives.*
*Nourish it then, that it may leaf and bloom and fill with singing birds."*
Black Elk

This reminds me of when an apple tree fell down on our property after a
heavy snow. We were so sad, and it seemed like it would not live.
Then, we had a gardener prop it back up and I prayed.
It lived! It flourishes! Each summer apples and birds fill the branches.

And isn't this like when we are drained emotionally, devoid of energy,
feeling like we can't go on; or are diagnosed with a life-threatening disease
or a dear loved one passes?

With some hope and a little faith and a big dose of love, we end up
thriving again. I am deeply grateful for resilience.

## – DAY 295 –

*"Trust where you came from . . . Trust where you are going . . .*
*Trust who you are . . . There are no mistakes, only opportunities*
*for you to know yourself even better."*
Frank Coppieters

I am cloaked in trust. I am filled with faith and assurance.
I absolutely know that wherever I have been, am now, or choose to go,
it is Divinely guided, even the times when it has seemed I was way off the
path of my spirituality.

So utterly and completely grateful for trusting in a Higher Power that is
always with me, guiding my way.

## – DAY 296 –

*"Morning has broken like the first morning*
*Blackbird has spoken like the first bird*
*Praise for the singing, praise for the morning*
*Praise for them springing fresh from the world."*
Cat Stevens

Thank you for this beautiful, spectacular, fantastic brand new day.

I am grateful to be alive.

I am grateful for my inner joy,
my inner peace,
and the light and love of Life expressing everywhere!

Part of what astounds me about life is the vastness
of all planes of existence.
There is so much more than imagination allows me to see.
Many years back, I had a tragedy in my life help me to lose some
skepticism I had; that let me discover that mediums are real;
that Edgar Cayce's intuitive healings are real; that the Akashic Records
are real; and that there is infinite energy and life everywhere.

Human life is just a dot in time, comparatively.

I am grateful, so grateful, to have opened my mind and heart to realms,
realms beyond physical senses and physical existence. It soothes my soul to
know that there is cosmic mystery, and unfathomable depths to life.

– DAY 298 –

*"Amazingly, as the infinite forms of flowers all rise from the same earth,
the earthly garden of emotions – all in their delicate shapes and colors –
all rise from the earth of the heart."*
Mark Nepo

Once I figured out that emotions always pass,
I truly honor every single emotion I experience – sad, mad, blah, elated,
excited, joyful and on and on . . . and I understand what Mark Nepo
means about how they arise like flowers, each unique and beautiful, really.

They bloom in passion, and then diminish.

I am grateful for the flowers of emotion in the garden of my heart.

*"Surrender isn't a sacrifice of the known,
but rather a celebration of the infinite."*
Nipun Mehta

It is such a gift to learn how to surrender to what is, to let go freely and
gracefully, to accept what is going on and not try to control.
And I find it amusing I used to think I could control the outside world
or people. Nope.
So it is actually practical to surrender.
When I surrender, I am knowing that the Divine has a plan;
and that way more is going on behind the scenes than my little mind
can comprehend.
I surrender to the Infinite – lovingly, joyously, again and again.

– DAY 300 –

*"You have to be able to imagine lives that are not yours."*
Wendell Berry

I am deeply grateful for growing compassion in my heart and soul.
It is true, though hard to accept sometimes, that everyone is doing the best
they can. Judgment of others is so counterproductive though tempting.

It helps to imagine a different life than mine. My time with alcohol and
drug abuse, which is over now, helps me to have some understanding
for those who are caught in that vicious cycle. Really listening and paying
attention to people around the world via media can help open my own
worldview. Realizing we are all so much alike despite our differences
helps. Hate breeds more hate. I am thankful to know all this and practice
loving-kindness and compassion as much as I can.

*"Soaking in the waters of gladness . . . assures us that we live in a world not only filled with violence and hate, but also stubbornly infused with Divine surprise, delicious moments, and a flow of freshness that can sustain us through the worst of times."*
Patricia Adams Farmer

I bask in the clear, calm waters of appreciation.
I don't deny the violence, separation and hatred going on,
but I do absolutely know that focusing on what I'm glad or grateful for
helps me navigate rough, turbulent waters.

It is absolutely grand to be gifted with amazing surprises, magic and newness. Thankful for this precious life.

# – DAY 302 –

*"If I contradict myself, I contradict myself.
I contain multitudes."*
Walt Whitman

Each of us is a mini-universe. We contain literal stardust in our bodies.
Cells and systems are multifarious within us.
We are deeper than we can even imagine.
We exist forever.

In this context, I know that if I change my mind, I change my mind.
So be it. I stand strong in integrity
and I allow myself the opportunity to change.
This is part of being a multidimensional being.
How amazing and wondrous we are way, way more than it seems.

## – DAY 303 –

*"Today, I celebrate my tiny shifts and incremental progress."*
Tama Kieves

I don't know about you, but I tend to push myself a lot.
"Get this done, and be sure to do that," I tell myself.
Often, I don't stop to congratulate myself on all that I do accomplish.
So, right now, I give myself a big break
and know that every step I take is in Divine order and timing.

Baby steps are grand!

I am always doing the very best I can.
And I am thankful to celebrate and love myself just as I am.

## – DAY 304 –

*"The little things? The little moments? They aren't little."*
Jon Kabat-Zinn

It's easy to miss the tiny blessings in my life.
To miss the microcosmic stuff, and focus on desiring big transformations
or gigantic miracles and shifts.

However, when I slow down and notice, truly everything is a miracle.
The greatest joy I feel comes from a sweet conversation or a good laugh,
or a walk in the magic forest around me, seeing miniscule wildflowers
sprouting, or appreciating the changing sky.
Enjoying the softness of my pup's fur when I pet her
or the devotion and love we share.
I am grateful for life, all aspects, big and little.

*"Confidence and love and the light of the world wait
below all the labors of our mind."*
Mark Nepo

One bane of being human is the overthinking I do. I let my logical mind
overtake me at times, and it loves to go wild!
That part of me most decidedly does not like being in the present
moment; and jumps around from past to future, grabbing for anything it
can gnaw on and there is always something.

The antidote is letting my heart guide me . . . as I let all the mental chatter
dissolve. I am incredibly grateful for the ways I know to quiet my mind –
spiritual tools of meditation, contemplation, listening to mystical music,
walking in nature, and going deep within, where peace, light and love abide.

– DAY 306 –

*"Who would deduce the dragonfly from the larva, the iris from the bud, the
lawyer from the infant? We are all shape-shifters and magical reinventors.
Life is really a plural noun, a caravan of selves."*
Diane Ackerman

Life is so magical, so awe-inspiring, so full of wonder.
I bow down in gratitude for the ability to grow, to learn,
to evolve, to change.
Aging gracefully is getting me to a place of true self-love, of letting go of
concerns about what others think.
I am so thankful for the shape-shifting going on everywhere around me,
and within me.

Life is splendiferous!

*"As the alchemist of your own life, find a little bit of the frequency you want to experience and place your attention there.*
*Pray from there. Affirm from there. Proclaim from there. Decree from there. Announce from there. And ultimately, as it becomes your perception of how you see Life, live from there."*
Michael B. Beckwith

Although we can't help sad and even horrible things that happen in our lives, we can react in a proactive way, one that helps us navigate out of unhappiness. A little bit of a pivot helps me so much. It changes my frequency and I can then pray, affirm, proclaim and decree from that higher-vibe place instead of feeling helpless and swayed by outside events. Cocreating with the Divine reaps rich rewards. I am thankful to know, believe and actualize this!

– DAY 308 –

*"By seeking goodness, being good, and affirming good,*
*you see this world as a garden of beauty."*
Paramahansa Yogananda

Even though I realize it's not "all good" as people sometimes blithely decree, I do absolutely believe that what we focus on, expands.

So, I consciously turn away from the negative spin of the media, or unkind people, focusing my attention on what is good and right with the world.
And there is so much!

I bask in the lovely garden of beauty within me and all around me.
I choose to live there.

*"Sufficiency isn't an amount at all. It is an experience, a context we generate, a declaration, a knowing that there is enough, that we are enough."*
Lynne Twist

I am constantly reminded there is enough, there is always, always enough. It makes me laugh at myself sometimes, when I am worried about money, and then a surprise payment comes in; or if I think we are out of a grocery item I need for a dish, and I look in our pantry, and there it is already! And as I am reminded, sufficiency and prosperity are so much more than having enough money. I am rich with family, friends, love, joy, peace, beauty, harmony and wisdom.

I AM GRATEFUL TO KNOW THE ABSOLUTE ABUNDANCE IN MY LIFE!

– DAY 310 –

*"Wholeness does not mean perfection. It means embracing brokenness as an integral part of life."*
Parker Palmer

All my life, I have been striving for perfection – in body, mind and spirit.

As I grow older and wise, I realize that I am actually already perfect, whole and complete,
with all of my qualities and all of my faults.

It is my intention now to accept my brokenness
along with my awesomeness.
And I am deeply thankful.

*"Being opened is the most difficult and rewarding part of being human."*
Mark Nepo

It is much easier for me to let myself close up, especially with bad news,
or a friend moving away, or a loved one dying.
It is my natural reaction to put barriers up so I don't feel so strongly.

Although it is easy for me to try to ignore or brush away loss, sadness and
sorrow, I know for sure it helps me be a more transparent, loving being
when I face whatever-it-is head-on.

In gratitude for being opened.

– DAY 312 –

*"If you wish to be something you are not – something fine, noble, good –
you shut your eyes and for one dreamy moment you are
that which you long to be."*
Helen Keller

Dreaming yields wonders.
And all manifestation starts with a dream.
How glorious it is to have free will and an active imagination.
Whatever I put into my mind, that makes sense for me, I can be.

I bravely dream of new frontiers, and then I take the steps
to actualize them.

I couldn't be more grateful for the potential and power of my dreams.

Today, I acknowledge the golden light of autumn.
I am in gratitude for this slowing-down season, a bridge to winter time.

As we step into a time of harvest, I reflect on all the bounty of this past year.
I am so grateful for the times I have spent with my dear family, those far away, and those right here with me including our pets!
I am so thankful for the joy and forgetting-of-time I relish at the river in the summer, and whenever I am immersed in nature.
I am thankful for every way I have grown in inner strength, love, peace and trust – through challenges, and through my daily contemplation.

I relish the abundant cornucopia of good that is my sacred life.

## – DAY 314 –

*"You are the brilliance and magnificent light of the Divine. Trust this.*
*Surrender to this, for it is the truth of your being."*
Eugene D. Holden

What an amazing concept, which becomes more true to me with each passing year, as I have grown into it.

It is true of me and it is true of you!
I am grateful to be harmonized, and part of the light of all creation.

I am in awe of the power that this gift allows me.
With this knowledge we can make the world a better place.
I'm in!

*"Nobody has all the answers. Knowing that you do not know everything*
*is far wiser than thinking you know a lot when you really don't."*
John Heider

How thankful I am to know I don't know. It is so freeing to simply say
"I don't know" when that is the truth.
I have known people who try to fake it, and act like a know-it-all.
In my youth, I was much more sure of everything. Life tends to humbles
us, though, and I am grateful to let myself be less arrogant as time passes.

It feels good to realize how vast the field of consciousness is, and to
answer when I know something, and stay quiet and listen when I do not.

– DAY 316 –

*"There's no limitation on love. There's no limitation on abundance.*
*There's no limitation on joy. There's no limitation on peace.*
*Rise up and go for it!"*
Michael B. Beckwith

How glad I am to feel unlimited, infinite abundance –
limitless joy and peace and harmony. It is always there, within us, we just
have to let go of worries and fear and embrace it!
I am happy to rise up and go for it!

I welcome in the plentitude of life in every way – dear family and friends,
money, inner peace, wholeness, well-being
and the all good of Spirit always.
Thankful beyond measure.

Today, I want to acknowledge the worlds upon worlds that exist,
from the macrocosms to the microcosms.

Every single square inch of our richly diverse Earth is filled with life –
above, below and on the surface.
We are giants to the mini worlds here.
And tiny, minute specks in the vast macrocosm of the cosmos.

I am in love with life, and in love with the fact that every single thing
IS alive. How wildly amazing.

I am more thankful than I can express for all life everywhere, and for my
own sacred, precious life.

## – DAY 318 –

*"Nothing can keep me from knowing the spiritual Truth.*
*No matter how loudly the world of effects roars around me,*
*I remain firmly planted in the fertile soil of spiritual Truth."*
Edward Viljoen

There is a visualization I do in my meditation time . . . I am standing
strong on my mountaintop of all good, giving and receiving all the
abundant blessings of life, which include peace, joy, prosperity, health,
love, creativity and harmony. This mountaintop is on a bedrock of faith
and trust with a gentle breeze of grace and ease blowing.

When I am on the mountaintop, the effects of the world do not shake me.
Always, again and again, I am so grateful for my spiritual path that
prompts me to know and remember the great good of God,
and our Oneness with it.

*"We are not the only ones affected by our recovery. The spiritual awakening
heals the world one person at a time."*
Marta Mrotek

Coming from a tough childhood and a hedonistic young adulthood,
it's like I have experienced two incarnations in one lifetime.

This second part of my life, I am incredibly grateful to be awake and aware.

I am positive that we can heal the world, one person at a time.
And I am certainly looking forward to a global heart awakening.

Light always shines away darkness,
and I am so thankful to do my part.

## – DAY 320 –

*"Since that day, I've never doubted the partnership between gratitude
and solution."*
David Ault

A superpowerful practice I use is to write thank you notes to the Divine
for what there is already to be grateful for,
and to always include what I am grateful for in advance.
I've been doing this for years – for a while it was daily, then weekly, and
now it is monthly. I watch in absolute delight as what I am thankful for in
the future comes to pass.

Spirit is not bounded by time.

*"In nature there is no alienation. Everything belongs."*
Deng Ming-Dao

We are the only ones in nature who feel separation, who can let ourselves feel alienated and alone. Every creature knows where they should be, and what they should do, and do not question the Divine order of their lives. I have come to realize the predators have their jobs to do, and that prey also have theirs. I do not judge the animals in nature anymore.

I know I belong, I know we all belong. I know there is Divine order in my own life. I believe strongly in the connection that exists among every single being, including humans. With all of our diversity, there is common ground. In our individuality, we still belong. Thank you, Spirit, for the grand creation of life on Earth and beyond.

– DAY 322 –

*"The threshold to all that is extraordinary in life opens only when we devote ourselves to giving attention, not getting it."*
Mark Nepo

I am so grateful to be a giver, not a getter.
When younger, I vied for attention, even choosing negative drama to be seen.

Now I'd rather step back and listen and pay attention.

When I do, life lights up! The extraordinary is revealed in every little thing. This lights up my heart and soul and nourishes me.

Yes, I am thankful.

*"But there's a shift happening in humanity, a shift in consciousness,
happening now because it has to happen now."*
Eckhart Tolle

From my hippie days in the 1960s, I have felt intuitively that I am called
to be here on Earth now, to be a part of a shift toward light, toward love,
toward peace in higher degrees than we have yet experienced.
I must say it is hard to believe sometimes! Darkness and violence and
hatred seem to engulf the world, and I can be dismayed and depressed
by it all. Yet, I still believe good things are already here, and that more
great good is on its way. All I have to do is refocus when I'm down, and
see what is going right, notice the kindness and love that abounds. And to
make sure I am operating at a high vibration, contributing to positivity,
and being those qualities I want to see.

– DAY 324 –

*"Be patient toward all that is unsolved in your heart
and try to love the questions themselves."*
Rainer Maria Rilke

I appreciate the mystery and the not-knowing of life.
I cherish the questions that present themselves to me,
even when I don't know the answers.

It wasn't always like this for me.
I let myself be impatient and I wanted to know when I wanted to know,
and it was unacceptable to live in uncertainty.

I honor myself for my growth and my willingness to know I don't know
and embrace accepting.

*"The heart is always the place to go. Go home into your heart,*
*where there is warmth, appreciation, gratitude and contentment."*
Ayya Khema

My heart is a safe haven. I let go of ego, and go home when I allow myself
to feel the pure love in my heart.

It is easy to go there, unless I am mad and even then, I let myself yield
and let go so I will feel better.

I believe that Spirit's messages are always loving, are always light-filled,
and so are the quiet messages from my caring, compassionate heart.

I love me, and I love the rest of the world! So thankful.

– DAY 326 –

*"What is life? It is the flash of a firefly in the night.*
*It is the breath of a buffalo in the wintertime. It is the little shadow which*
*runs across the grass and loses itself in the sunset."*
Chief Crowfoot

I embrace life, and know that life is in every small moment, in and through
every single living presence on this Earth and beyond.

I feel the love in the cool breeze,
the baby squirrels playing on our land right now,
in the wise old trees surrounding us, in the twinkling stars at night.

Thank you, Life, for your infinite manifestations!

*"Peace is the generous, tranquil contribution of all to the good of all.
Peace is dynamism. Peace is generosity. It is right and it is duty."*
Óscar Romero

My cup runneth over with gratitude for all the times when I feel the deep
well of peace saturating my heart and soul.
I dwell there often in my morning meditation time,
and consciously I bring it back to me when I sometimes lose it
during day-to-day life.

Thank you, Spirit, for abiding peace.
As we all learn to feel it and know it and reside in that wellspring of calm
composure, where we don't let our feathers be ruffled so easily,
our world will be a much more harmonious place!

*"What don't you get about forever?"*
The Group

How glad I am to have a belief system that lets me trust that there is
more, much more, to us than this temporal world.
I am grateful to feel eternity in my heart and soul.
It helps so much when someone I dearly love passes to believe that we
will meet again somehow, some way.

I know for sure there is way more going on than what appears,
and I am so appreciative of the mysteries and enigmas I can't understand.

Life is a vast amazing wonderland, and stretches from universe to universe
and beyond.

## – DAY 329 –

*"The key word for our time is practice.*
*We have all the light we need, we just need to put it into practice."*
Peace Pilgrim

I am grateful for practice, practice, practice.

Life always helps me exercise practice in many ways,
practicing more lovingkindness, toward myself and others,
and practicing acceptance as I grow older.

And how thankful I am for my daily spiritual practice.
And for the knowledge that we have already everything we need even
when it might not seem so. Thank you, Life, for providing light, love,
peace, joy and abundance. I keep my lantern lit.

## – DAY 330 –

*"She quietly expected great things to happen to her,*
*and no doubt that's one of the reasons why they did."*
Zelda Fitzgerald

I am always grateful for the concept that what we expect transpires as we
cocreate with the Universe.

I watch as it happens in my life so bountifully.

When I doubt or worry or fear, though, I can cancel out the good on its way.

So thankful to live in trust and the knowing that there is a beneficial
Presence within me and everyone. We are actually powerful beyond
knowing, and I give great thanks for that.

I am thankful for learning lessons about surrender.
I'm in awe at how Michael A. Singer has made it his life's work to let go of attachment to how he thinks things should be, and instead has total and complete trust that life always leads him in the best directions.

If I'm honest, I definitely struggle with this concept.
A trivial matter can set me off for the rest of the day, because I hold on to it and can't seem to let go. I am not always clear if I should take action on a matter, or how it might be better to simply let go and just let life happen.

With meditation and contemplation as strongholds in my life, I surrender more easily and give myself a break for being a "work in progress."
I am grateful for gentle acceptance of myself, and life in general.

## – DAY 332 –

*"The winter solstice has always been special to me as a barren darkness that gives birth to a verdant future beyond imagination,
a time of pain and withdrawal that produces something joyfully inconceivable, like a monarch butterfly masterfully extracting itself from the confines of its cocoon, bursting forth into unexpected glory."*
Gary Zukav

I give great thanks for all the seasons, each offering their own special gifts.
I am glad for the winter solstice, which is the darkest day/night of the year, and I do look forward to more and more light as we head toward spring not so far away.

Let us honor winter for snow, rain, wood fires and a toasty home, for snuggling, and extra blankets on the bed. Cozy in the warmth of gratitude.

*"When you are right, everything around you is right, for the beautiful flow
that is inside your heart has the capacity to spread its fragrance
of Oneness-light all around you."*
Sri Chinmoy

That feeling of all-is-well floods my being and spreads out to all
I come in contact with.

I am wildly blessed and grateful beyond measure for the peace and
harmony within me that floods my daily existence with its goodness.

I know light and love are all-pervasive and catching.
Thank you, Universe.

– DAY 334 –

*"The desire to reach for the stars is ambitious.
The desire to reach hearts is wise."*
Maya Angelou

How glad I am to let go of blind ambition, to quit comparing, and trying to
get ahead no matter what. With aging, comes sweetening and mellowing
out. With aging, comes altruism.

With aging, comes appreciating what is really important in life,
which is reaching out with love freely, and being kind.

And this must include treating my own self with compassion too.

I am thankful to be aging gracefully.

## – DAY 335 –

*"During times of quiet contemplation, I bring to mind everything
I have to be grateful for, and those thoughts fill my mind like wildflowers
blooming in a field."*
Unity Daily Word, October 27, 2020

Today, right now, my heart is filled to the brim with gratitude, my mind is
overflowing with thankful thoughts.

The joy vibration is strong, the peace vibration is steady, when I am feeling
this way. And I rejoice!

Let me remember to cultivate gratitude within so my joy and peace
quotients are blooming abundantly like a wildflower extravaganza.

## – DAY 336 –

*"Reality is permeated, indeed flooded, with Divine creativity,
nourishment, and care."*
Marcus J. Borg

I am grateful beyond measure for the miracle of life!
Even when it might not seem so, I feel and know that we are nourished
and cared for by the All-in-All.

Looking at each individual person, gazing at all the myriad creatures,
observing the seasons and the countless stars in the sky, it is obvious and
undeniable that there IS Divine creativity that abounds.

And that is enough to sustain me and help me to grow in my faith of the
good of life. So thankful.

*"There wells up from within us a trust, a consciousness that we are surrounded by an Infinite Goodness . . . Let our lives be peaceful; let our lives be whole. Then shall that Peace which is God abiding within us radiate from us."*
Ernest Holmes

How grateful I am to feel the Infinite Goodness
so that I can easily release fear and doubt when I go there.

Oh, yes, I remember! Spirit's got this! It is not up to li'l ol' me.

Then I am filled with serenity, grace and a deep peace
as I surrender all my petty grievances and wants and desires
knowing that there is a grander plan than I can possibly imagine.
And I am infinitely thankful.

– DAY 338 –

*"There is much to be thankful for each day. Every Dawn as it comes is a holy event and everyday is holy."*
Roy Cook

As I woke up this morning, and saw the tangerines and pinks of the morning sun rising, I felt hope and optimism, and felt that this was a sign.

It truly is a miracle and blessing to wake up to each new day.

And the beauty of creation is beyond phenomenal.

Today, right now, I am so grateful for new beginnings, the dawn of more
love and peace and harmony in the world
that is surely coming.

*"A swan glides across the water gracefully with its beautiful white feathers and long, slender neck. It is a symbol of grace. Under the surface, its feet paddle to maintain momentum to keep the swan afloat.*
*Grace takes work."*
Emily Silva

Oh, it is so amazing how things are not always what they appear on the surface. Each of us a masterpiece of creation, and each of us have struggles that don't always show.

I am incredibly grateful for grace and beauty.
I am thankful for mystery and magic and awe.

Life is truly astounding.

– DAY 340 –

*"I fast from all ideas of lack and feast on the idea of abundance."*
Ernest Holmes

Mother Nature in all her glory is a constant reminder
of the abundance of the universe.

I allow myself to be reminded, again and again, that there is always,
yes, always enough!

My life is filled with rich plenty – plenty of love, plenty of friends,
plenty of nature's spectacular beauty, plenty of joy, of peace, of all-is-well.
I am rich and I am fulfilled in every way.
And I am deeply thankful.

## – DAY 341 –

*"In each of us there is a spark that can reverse the trends of violence and depression spiraling within us and in the world around us. By setting in motion the spiral of gratefulness we begin the journey toward peace and joy."*
Br. David Steindl-Rast

Today, I give great thanks for the spark I feel within,
that joy spark, that happiness spark, that peace spark
that emanates from my heart and soul whenever I let all petty worries and
concerns go.

All that truly matters is our Divine connection to Spirit
and the love we share.
How truly grand it is to let my sparks of gratitude fly!

## – DAY 342 –

*"Practicing contentment is a radical act in a consumption-driven society."*
Robin Wall Kimmerer

I have read testimonials by those who were evacuated during wildfires and
firestorms who said what they learned is that the stuff doesn't matter.
And I do remember this well when we were evacuated because of a fire.
What matters, really matters, is the people and creatures who are our
family and friends; and savoring the abundance of nature that doesn't cost
a penny; and the love and contentment that is only found within despite
anything crazy/upsetting/maddening going on in this world.

I am grateful to have my priorities straight so that I'm clear that getting
material extras is truly not that important.
I am thankful to be radically grateful.

*"We can never underestimate this truth:*
*No matter who you are, the biggest thing you do in any day*
*is most often going to be a small act of kindness, decency, or love."*
Cory Booker

So thankful to give from my heart, as much as possible.
Being kind and being loving is a priority for me
and though I don't always succeed,
I do pretty darn good most of the time.

I am in gratitude for all the sweet role models in my life,
teaching me and showing me the way.

# – DAY 344 –

The people in my life who are gracious and kind win my heart.
They seem to know just the right thing to say, diplomatically,
even in uncomfortable situations.

I am grateful to learn from each of them through the years.

I am thankful for civility, for respecting other's viewpoints
even when diametrically opposed.

I am thankful for listening and caring what another says before
interrupting. I can be surprised what someone says if I listen rather than
blurt out my opinion before they are done.

Let me be as gracious and kind as I can be, always. Thank you, God.

*"It is not the strongest of the species that survives, nor the most intelligent.
It is the one that is most adaptable to change."*
Charles Darwin

Change is definitely a constant occurrence in life. I didn't expect the
COVID 2020 pandemic to bring such a disruption to our routines!
And I found myself adapting better and better as the months went by.
I am thankful, truly thankful, to accept change, realizing it will come and
keep coming. If I want to be peaceful, I will accept it.

Sometimes change is fantastic!
And often change, even when I resist, ends up bringing about a higher
good than I could ever imagine.
I am grateful to flow with change.

– DAY 346 –

*"The whole world is an art gallery when you're mindful. There are beautiful
things everywhere and they're free."*
Charles Tart

When I look around, I see beauty in every nook and cranny, near and far.
I've always believed God is the most amazing artist there is –
from giraffes and chameleons; to the paintbrush of colors that wash over
each season; to madrones and oaks, to the teeniest weed coming up
through a crack in a sidewalk. And of course, the endless starry nights and
hope-filled rosy hues of dawn. The variety of artwork is infinite.

And each person is a Divine creation.
Beauty on the outside, yes, but most of all, beauty on the inside.
With an open heart, with an open mind, each person is beauty expressing.
And I am so thankful for every bit of God's artwork.

*"May those whose hell it is to hate and hurt be turned into lovers bringing flowers."*
Shantideva

At this time, let all love bloom!
I am guilty sometimes of hating, and it never feels right.
It brings me down because it is not a natural state for us humans.

Divinity is love. I am one with Divinity.
And I let anything unlike love and kindness melt away
and purposely keep my heart open.

I pray that peace, unity, harmony and love spread throughout
the land, and prevail.

## – DAY 348 –

*"Be humble for you are made of Earth. Be noble for you are made of stars."*
Serbian Proverb

We are all so much alike, with so much more in common
than I often realize.

It is a scientific (and truly magical) fact that we are composed partially of
ancient stardust, and we are inextricably linked with the earth, the seas,
the air, the water.
I feel humble to know this, and I honor my Divinity too.

How grateful I am to feel the deep connection
that holds this universe together.
WE ARE ONE!

## – DAY 349 –

Around every corner can be an unexpected blessing.

With the gray doldrums of wintertime, comes our seasonal creek
a'flowing, rivulets cascading into waterfalls.

How grateful I am for surprises and gifts from the Universe.

I pay attention, and there they are.

Kindnesses, gratitude, love . . . and stunningly beautiful,
wondrous nature.

## – DAY 350 –

*"Doubt is an uncomfortable condition, but certainty is a ridiculous one."*
Voltaire

I have been so absolutely sure of my stance on something,
only to have it proven wrong later.

To really know I don't know is invaluable.
This world and all the planes of existence are filled with mystery
and I delight in not knowing it all.

Uncertainty leads to discovery.
I am grateful to be a sojourner into parts unknown.

*"If you want the rainbow, you gotta put up with the rain."*
Dolly Parton

I am so thankful for my courage, for my fortitude,
for my inner tenacity of Spirit.

As outside circumstances at times dampen my optimism,
I go within and summon up my bravery.

And in so doing, I find the positivity and gratitude that is never far away.
I welcome it and luxuriate in the inner well of good and God within me.

## – DAY 352 –

*"I like living. I have sometimes been wildly, despairingly, acutely miserable,
racked with sorrow, but through it all I still know quite certainly
that just to be alive is a great thing."*
Agatha Christie

Life IS beautiful and although we face some challenges in this time on
Earth, I know that all things shift and change in the temporal world,
and I am grateful to be here, right now.

It is precious and sacred to be alive. I feel it and proclaim that.

And my thankful thoughts keep me on the right track, for sure.

Feeling infinitely supported,
I row gently, gently down the stream of life letting go of expectations,
trusting in the benevolence of the universe . . .
safe and secure and serene.

I am grateful for a silent partnership with the Infinite!

The still, small voice is always whispering wisdom
when I get quiet and listen.

– DAY 354 –

*"Find the balance in the center and you will live in harmony."*
Michael A. Singer

Earlier in my life, I tended toward extremes.
Balance, the Middle Way, and discipline didn't speak to my rebel
hedonistic heart, and I still tend to go full-tilt boogie into the things I love.

Nowadays I am totally focused on my spiritual path and meditation and
prayer, which actually lead to more balance.

I bow to balance.
I embrace balance in my life in every way.
I am so grateful for feeling balanced and purposely being balanced in my
mind, body and spirit. Harmony prevails.

*"Surf through experiences and conditions by asking what is a greater expression of life in this area? Live in that question, and waves of insight will become more available to you."*
Michael B. Beckwith

We are going through many challenges right now as the human race, sometimes it feels like too much to bear. Obvious climate-change weather occurrences, so much division and hatred between factions.

In my meditation time, I ask myself "What is a greater expression of life in this area?" And what comes to me is that through what we don't want, we are getting clearer on what we do. All of these are conditions and experiences shall pass. I am one with nature, nature is one with me.
I am love and harmony and unity. Amen!

– DAY 356 –

I am open to receive a beautiful even flow
of incoming gifts from the Universe,
and to give in great measure too.

The light of generosity is shining to me, through me,
and reaching outward.

My life is plentiful, I am a giver of good,
and I am so thankful.

*"Those who contemplate the beauty of the Earth find reserves of strength that will endure as long as life lasts."*
Rachel Carson

I always find solace in the nature around me, in the sacred beauty of where I live.

I am so very grateful to live near rivers, in the forest, near the powerful, vast Pacific Ocean.

It makes me strong to live each day seeped in the wonder and magic of Mother Nature. Thankful beyond measure for all of creation.

# – DAY 358 –

*"The world is shifting, awakening. As we become better stewards of ourselves, we are better stewards of the world.
Sharing the love we are, the healing begins."*
Jane Beach

I am deeply grateful for my own self-care.
As I keep myself vital and healthy in all ways – physically, emotionally, mentally and spiritually,
I know I am expanding my loving presence.

Because I am the only one I can change and improve, I am thankful to let this sink in deeper and deeper as life goes on.

I am thankful for my new motto: "I do me and you do you!"

## – DAY 359 –

*"The spaciousness love creates can feel as vast as the ocean's depths. Let love be fluid. Let the rising and falling occur, knowing that love is endless."*
Emily Silva

Love is so infinite when my heart is open.
I feel deep unconditional love for myself, for all others,
when I can release judgment – a challenge sometimes, for sure.
Let me love, let me love in a wholly, holy way, as Rickie Byars Beckwith's
beautiful song invites us. Let us all love more and more, and let go of the
divisiveness that holds us back from being love incarnate.

It is an incredible gift to love, to be loved, and to know it.
Thank you, Loving Presence.

## – DAY 360 –

*"Pay attention to the beckoning whispers of the things you love to do
as well as to your dreams and visions."*
Sanaya Roman

I am thankful to listen to my inner self, filled with wisdom,
filled with love, filled with hopes and dreams, and creative fulfillment.

I don't ignore the whispers I hear ever so faintly,
that still small voice within.

And I celebrate that I hear, and then often take action.

*"Love your edges because they point the way to freedom.*
*Let yourself fall through into the infinite. That's what it means to go beyond."*
Michael A. Singer

How good it is to know that my rough edges, the thorns that poke me, are a part of me, but do not have to rule me. I am so thankful to be aware of the prickly parts of myself that show me where I can soften and keep my heart open instead of closing.

How grand it is to let myself fall through into the infinite,
because each of us is so much more than our personality and ego.
In the bigger picture, we are spinning in space on a beautiful jewel of a planet
and the things I choose to make a big deal really aren't.

– DAY 362 –

*"Although we have been made to believe that*
*if we let go we will end up with nothing,*
*life reveals just the opposite: that letting go*
*is the real path to freedom."*
Sogyal Rinpoche

I am so grateful for the realization that letting go and surrendering
is a true blessing in my life.
I can be so sure I know what an outcome should be;
I can be so proactive in making this outcome happen;
and then when life takes a surprise turn instead and it doesn't happen,
I am almost always delightfully surprised to see what transpires instead of
my own ego-driven plans!
I let go and I let God.

*"So it is totally wrong to say that the practice of tolerance and practice of forgiveness are signs of weakness. Totally wrong. Hundred percent wrong. Thousand percent wrong. Forgiveness is a sign of strength."*
Dalai Lama

The strongest role models I know practice radical forgiveness, such as the Dalai Lama, for his exile from his homeland. May I learn from the great leaders of our world, and also the common amazing person who is able to forgive, even when there has been great harm done to them or their family.

I am grateful to understand that forgiveness sets me free, and holding on to grievances binds me. I forgive all who I feel need my forgiveness, and that includes myself. And I forgive again and again as needed.
I am gentle and loving and strong!

I am thankful for all the encouragement I have received in my life – from my "cheerleader" mother; teachers who believed in me and praised me highly; and those who are mentors to me now – including wise friends; awe-inspiring authors and leaders, both current and from the distant past, who I many times quote in my gratitude passages.

And I am also grateful for those I am honored to teach; to those I am honored to inspire and mentor; to those I know who join me on a growing, meandering spiritual path too.

It feels so good to pay it forward.

*"Everything is a gift. The degree to which we are awake to this truth is a measure of our gratefulness, and gratefulness is a measure of our aliveness."*
Br. David Steindl-Rast

I am grateful for the practice of radical gratitude . . .
meaning that when tough times come, or something goes seriously awry,
I look for the blessing in it. I look for what it is teaching me.

It may take time to find what is a gift about a situation,
but it is always revealed.

And it is not always easy to be thankful for trials and challenges,
but it is possible. I stand strong with a grateful, open heart no matter
what. And I am thankful to be fully alive.

## DEBORAH PERDUE

teaches spiritual classes, and facilitates workshops and retreats on the
topics of gratitude, abundance and how to live a life of joy. As well as
authoring several books, she publishes blogs and articles on inner peace
and gratitude which can be found at www.graceofgratitude.com.

Deborah has been a licensed practitioner for the Centers for Spiritual Living
since 2006. She is also a freelance book designer.

She lives in the forest of beautiful Southern Oregon in a dome home
with her husband and menagerie.

*It is Deborah's calling and intention to continue
to expand the potent spiritual practice of
gratitude in the world!*

GO TO

# www.GraceOfGratitude.com

to order

more products including

two beautiful Gratitude Journals,

*Daily Gratitude Reflections Volume 1,*

coloring books

and gorgeous greeting cards.


Sign up for Daily Gratitude Reflections at info@graceofgratitude.com


*Your Opinion Matters*

I hope you enjoyed reading my book.

**Your feedback on Amazon is very important to me and it**

**also helps others determine if this book is right for them.**

Would you please go to Amazon and leave feedback

for this book now? It would be so helpful

and very much appreciated.

Thank you!

CPSIA information can be obtained
at www.ICGtesting.com
Printed in the USA
BVHW051235131221
623894BV00021B/848